# AN
# ACCIDENTAL
# AMERICAN

Memories of an Immigrant Childhood

## Ruth Stern Gasten

**To order additional copies of this book, contact:**
Xlibris Corporation
1-888-795-4274
www.Xlibris.com
Orders@Xlibris.com
74926

# An
# Accidental
# American

# Contents

# DEDICATION

To young people who want to learn what life was like in the "old country" and then what life was like for immigrants like me when we came to the "new country."

To people of all ages who want to pay a visit to turbulent times.

# Special Thanks

This book was prompted by questions from my grandchildren. It was started in the writing class of Nancy O'Connell at Las Positas College, whose knowledge and encouragement have been of enormous help in the process. I am grateful to Mary Adamson and Judy Barnett for their insights and critiques of my work. Hector Timourian and Rick Altman were of great assistance by instructing me in self-publishing.

I am grateful to my daughter, Amy Gasten Shenon, and son-in-law, Michael Shenon, for trusting me to take their children back to the "old country."

My Nieder-Ohmen cousin, Karola Stern Steinhardt, and Werner Cohen, Cousin Hilda's husband, were of help by checking my memories of long ago events. Historical information on the town came from Hilda's book, *Words that Burn Within Me*.

Heinrich Reighel, the Nieder-Ohmen historian, allowed me to use photographs from his books (including the Stern Family Home and German soldiers) and provided valuable insights into the village of my youth.

My family and friends were wonderfully patient with me during this long process. They read stories willingly and made useful comments. I appreciate it. My partner, Sam Stone, gave me loving support and cooked many a dinner while I worked away at the computer. I couldn't have done it without all your help!

# Prologue

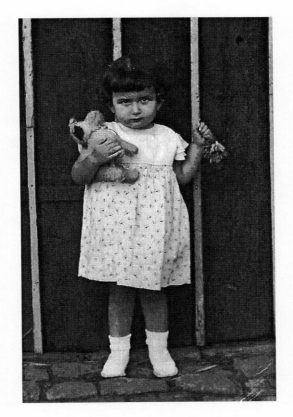

Little Ruthie, Age Two (1935)

Hitler and I entered the world scene in the same year—1933. He came to power, and I was born to Joseph Stern, a cattle dealer, and his wife, Hanna, who lived in the tiny town of Nieder-Ohmen, Germany, population 1,400.

Germany was going through tumultuous times. Runaway inflation caused job loss and financial ruin for many people. Because of the economic and social problems, the Nazi movement took hold immediately with some people in town—particularly the young men and boys. They felt there might be something new and exciting happening in the country and eagerly joined the *Hitler Jugend* (Hitler Youth).

Being Jewish, my parents soon became aware that the Hitler regime was using the Jews as scapegoats to explain the country's problems. My father's family had lived in Nieder-Ohmen for over 200 years. They were known and liked by the community, and my father was sure the decent people of his town would protect his family. My mother, not being from the town, was not so sure and became more frightened everyday by what she saw happening around her.

My mother came from Ulmbach, another small town about one hundred miles away. Her father had died in 1919, and her six brothers had scattered to larger communities by the time Hitler started his anti-Semitic campaign. They had seen how serious it was. One by one, in the mid-thirties, they left Germany for other countries. Four of them and my grandmother, Fannie, immigrated to South Africa. One went to live in Southern Rhodesia, now Zimbabwe. Another found a new home in Palestine, now Israel.

Her brothers had pleaded with my parents to leave Germany, but my father's faith in his country and his friends in Nieder-Ohmen kept him and his brother there. After all, they had both served honorably in the German army in World War I. Surely, their valor and their love of their homeland would count in their favor.

If my parents had made different choices, I might have become "An Accidental South African" or "An Accidental Israeli" instead of "An Accidental American." What different lives I might have led!

This book is about my first ten years—years of upheaval, tension, sadness, and adventure that brought me from quiet Nieder-Ohmen to the big, bustling city of Chicago, Illinois, to begin a new life in the United States.

I want future generations hear our stories, but not so they can hate the Germans. Far from it! My own experiences in Germany show that we must not condemn an entire people for the actions of some. The stories need to be told so that we can learn from the past. My dream is that future generations will stand up and speak out if they see injustice and prejudice arise in the land. I envision a world where *each* person is valued for their strengths and is given a chance to use them.

# The Story of Hanna

My mother, Johanna Nussbaum, was born in 1898, the second child of Meier and Fannie Nussbaum, the only girl with six brothers. She grew up in one of the few Jewish families in Ulmbach, a small town in central Germany. My mother wistfully told me, "I worked hard as a little girl. Your *Oma* (Grandma) Fannie and I cleaned the house, washed and ironed the clothes, cooked and served the food. When everyone had eaten, and we were so tired, *Oma* and I did the dishes and put them away. My brothers worked outdoors with *Opa* (Grandpa) Meier, but also had time to play card games, see their friends, and read books. Think about it. There were six of them to help with the "men's" work and only one to help with the "women's" work." I sensed the envy in her voice as she compared her life with her brothers'.

Hanna attended the local school until eighth grade. When the priest came to the school every day and led the students in their prayers, the Jewish children waited outdoors. From the time she started school, she learned that she and her fellow Jews were outsiders, literally and figuratively. What would make a child feel like an outsider more than being asked to wait outside while the rest of the children participated in a learning that was not part of your heritage?

Mama recounted, "In the long German winters, those prayer sessions seemed to go on forever. It was so cold. We could see our breath when we talked. We wore mittens; still, our fingers felt like icicles."

Hanna was a smart girl, good in her studies. Even though she was busy at home and didn't spend much time doing homework, her grades were excellent. Yet girls from small rural communities in Germany had no chance for a high school education. There was no high school in Ulmbach, and no money to send her to a larger city. So, Hanna remained at home and helped with the "women's" work.

There was always something to do around the Nussbaum house. Fridays were especially busy. After all, the women of the house had to get ready for *Shabbat* (the Sabbath). Mama and *Oma* Fannie baked two large *challahs*, (the twisted egg bread eaten on Friday evening and Saturday), a large batch of cookies, and two cakes. Then it was time to make chicken soup—a Friday afternoon ritual. When the chicken had flavored the soup, *Oma* Fannie would pick the pieces out of the white enamel soup pot and add them to the large black iron roaster into which Hanna had cut up carrots, onions, turnips, and potatoes.

At sundown, *Oma* Fannie lighted the candles and said the blessing, which officially started the celebration of Shabbat. The Jewish laws prohibited any work being done until three stars were visible in the night sky on Saturday evening. Therefore, enough food was made on Friday to feed all nine of the Nussbaums for a full day. After all, the large family had to eat a hearty Saturday afternoon meal. With six growing boys, they needed to prepare lots of food, which was all eaten up by sundown on Saturday.

Then there were seasonal holidays. Passover created the most work. It happened in the spring, March or April, depending on the lunar cycle. Mama and *Oma* Fannie did their spring-cleaning just before Passover. Not only did they scrub the floors, the cabinets, beat the rugs, and scour the sink and stove, but they removed every tiny morsel of bread and grain from the cupboards. Why, you might wonder? It's all because of the Exodus. When Moses led the Jews out of Egypt to escape slavery, there was no time for their bread dough to rise. The desert sun baked it into flat matzohs. To celebrate the escape, one week a year observant Jews eat only matzohs—nothing made with yeast or any other grain that swells, such as rice, barley, oats, or rye. As a child, I could understand the prohibition against yeast, but not being able to eat rice or barley puzzled me. It still does.

The Nussbaum family did not question the rules. They obeyed them. After the house was spotlessly clean, *Oma* Fanny called to her sons, "Hurry now! Up to the attic and bring down all the boxes marked Passover". Goodness! What a lot of boxes! Some contained two sets of dishes—one for dairy and the other for meat meals. Some held the pots, pans, and baking sheets. Two small boxes were filled with sets of cutlery—the dairy set and the meat set. Hanna and *Oma* Fanny set to work removing the everyday dishes, pans and cutlery from the cupboards, putting them into empty boxes brought down from the attic and replacing them with the Passover dishes, pots and pans, and cutlery. Eating on the Passover tablecloths and using the Passover dishes while sampling the specially prepared Passover foods was a delightful change for the whole family, except for Hanna and *Oma* Fannie who were worn out when the whole switching process was finally complete.

We haven't even talked about the preparations for the two Passover Seders yet. "*Seder*" means telling. Each year Jewish families prepare a ceremonial dinner, which symbolizes the flight from Egypt, the journey from slavery to freedom. First of all, the Seder plate must be readied. It is a large round plate with decorative paintings in six small circles to tell you what goes where. You need a roasted lamb bone, some grated horseradish, *charoset* {chopped apples and nuts), cut up parsley, an egg, and salt water in a bowl. Nowadays you can buy grated horseradish, but Mama's brothers would take turns grating it until there was enough for both Seders. They complained, "This horseradish is strong enough to take the enamel off our teeth," and playfully moaned and groaned.

Gefilte fish was an important part of the Passover meal. The chopped fish appetizer originated in the Middle Ages because the Jews were too poor to serve whole fish. The housewives figured out a way to use inexpensive freshwater fish, and stretch them by chopping them and adding fillers so that everyone could at least have a taste. Oma Fannie had a huge well-worn wooden bowl and a chopper. First she chopped three different kinds of fish and onions together. Then she added eggs, matzo meal, and spices. Finally, she formed the mixture into ovals that were dropped into the fish broth simmering on the stove and cooked them for two hours. While she was working on the fish, Mama would season the beef briskets and cut up the vegetables for the *tzimmes (a savory meat and vegetable roast)* and grate the onions and potatoes for the potato kugel. Since you couldn't start the cooking until you had set up the Passover kitchen, all of it had to be done in one frantically busy afternoon. What a huge job!

Mama dreamed of leaving Ulmbach and going somewhere lively where she could wear pretty dresses, go dancing, and meet young men who weren't related to her. She heard of a Jewish hotel in Bad Nauheim, a health resort known for its salt springs, where young girls could work while learning how to set a beautiful table, decorate a room, and other skills to help in being a gracious homemaker. Mama pleaded with *Oma*, "Please, please can I apprentice there? I know I will learn a lot. I'll bring home new tasty recipes for us to try!"

*Oma* was torn. *Opa* Meier had died in the flu epidemic of 1919, and she relied on her conscientious daughter for help and moral support. On the other hand, she knew there was no future for Hanna in Ulmbach. *Oma* sighed, wiped a tear from her eyes and bravely said, "I'll miss you, but I know it's the right thing to do." By this time, her sons were also leaving for apprenticeships in other towns. Life at the Nussbaum house was simpler, and *Oma* wanted her daughter to learn new skills, meet new people, and have a chance to enjoy her youth.

Hanna was on her knees scrubbing the kitchen floor and humming the Johann Strauss waltz, "Tales from the Vienna Woods". Visions of handsome young men in trim summer suits and pretty girls in pastel evening gowns gaily dancing together in an elegant ballroom floated through her head. She saw the ballroom with its crystal chandelier, the polished wooden floors, and the tall red velvet draped windows that circled the room. For her, going to Bad Nauheim was like going to Vienna would be for you or me—a magical place with beautiful hotels and large stately mansions where dreams could come true.

Hanna wrote to the Bad Nauheim hotel asking for a position. A month later, the mailman brought an official looking letter to Hanna. She was so excited that she had trouble opening the envelope. By then, her mother was looking over her shoulder.

Together they read, "*Liebe Fraulein* Nussbaum: "We have an opening for an apprentice position on May 1.

We offer it to you. Please let us know if you can accept it. Hotel Weidman, Ella Weidman "

Hanna hugged her mother and twirled her around. What a sight! Hanna in her black stockings, print pinafore apron over her navy blue cotton skirt and white blouse, and her mother dressed in a gray baggy dress and wearing her "*sheidel*" (the severe wig worn by Orthodox Jewish married women who did not show their hair)—the two of them doing a spontaneous dance in the kitchen, much to the amusement of the two youngest boys, Leo and Siegfried.

So much to be done before May 1! New underwear had to be purchased. Hanna and her mother decided to make a stylish dress for her urban life in Bad Nauheim. She looked at all the fabric in the local store and bought some soft green and white polka dot cotton, which Oma cut out and sewed into a full-skirted dress with a V neckline and short sleeves. Hanna tried it on when it was finished and loved what she saw—a slim girl with gray green eyes and brown curly hair wearing a pretty dress that made her eyes look more green than gray. She was a happy young woman.

Departure day finally arrived—a sunny day with gentle breezes blowing through the tall trees that surrounded the Nussbaum home. Everyone was going to walk to the train station with Hanna. All six of the boys came home for the occasion. What a sight they were on the train platform! The boys were in their heavy wool tweed Sabbath suits, looking warm and uncomfortable. Jakob carried Hanna's brown fake leather suitcase. Hanna and Oma stood close together arm-in-arm. Oma was wearing her best black dress. Since she had been widowed, she wore black when she went out. Her children hoped she'd stop doing that since Opa Meier had been dead for over two years, and they wanted Oma to start enjoying her life again. If they had been able to see into the future, they would have been sad, because she never did.

Hanna, small, slim, and energetic, looked like a delicate spring flower in her pale blue cotton dress. Her oval face was surrounded by wavy brown hair that had been bobbed by Oma to imitate a hairstyle that Hanna had seen in a newspaper photo. There she was, darting from brother to brother, giving each instructions about household chores, reminding them of jobs that needed doing in the vegetable garden which was so important to the meals of the Nussbaum family.

"Don't worry, Hanna, I guarantee that the house will still be standing when you return, and there will be food to eat. We'll take care of things," reassured Jakob, her older brother.

Suddenly, a soft noise in the distance got louder and louder and turned into a roar as the train approached the station. No other passengers were getting on the train that sunny Sunday morning. The boys' chatter stopped as they watched the train slow down. White clouds of smoke spewed out of the imperious black engine. The boys loved trains and waved to the engineer sitting high in the cab. He jovially waved back. The train whistle alerted everyone that the train was about to stop. *Oma* Fannie started weeping quietly, but Hanna barely noticed. She could hardly contain her anticipation and excitement. What was her life going to be like in glamorous, lively Bad Nauheim?

The train made many stops in all the small towns along the tracks. Hanna distractedly looked out the train window at the wheat and cornfields, and green pastures with cows grazing placidly, but she just wanted to get there. After what seemed like hours, the conductor called out "Bad Nauheim!" Hanna grabbed her suitcase and rushed off the train and into the ornate train station with its stained glass windows, high ceilings and beautiful pastel colored tiles on the floor.

A smiling young woman with bobbed red hair and a spotless white dress hurried up to Hanna and said, "I'm Ella Weidman from Hotel Weidman. You must be Hanna Nussbaum. Let me take your suitcase, and we'll walk to the hotel."

Hanna took a deep breath as she saw the wide street in front of the station. On both sides were two and three-story highly decorated white buildings with burnt orange tile roofs. Many of them had "Hotel" signs on them. She saw balconies with flower boxes filled with red and pink geraniums on the second and third floors.

Ella asked Hanna if she had ever been to Bad Nauheim before. Hanna answered shyly, "No, this is my first time here, but I've heard that many people come here to take the baths and their health improves."

"Yes, that's true," responded Ella. "In 1869 two doctors discovered that the saline baths and exercises they developed help people with heart and nerve diseases. So, the clinics were built, and Nauheim became *Bad* (spa) Nauheim. People from all over Europe and even the United States visit the spa. You'll enjoy being in this lovely town, Hanna."

Hanna's eyes sparkled as she nodded her head up and down and exclaimed, "Oh yes! I know I will."

The two young women walked four blocks from the station and turned the corner to a pleasant tree-lined street. Hanna saw a tasteful brass sign that read "Hotel Weidman" fastened to the front of a spacious white wooden building with a large front porch. People were sitting in wicker chairs on the porch, chatting and smiling. *What a friendly house,* she thought. *I'm going to like it here.*

Ella showed Hanna to her third floor room. When Hanna swung open the door, she saw a small walnut dresser complete with a mirror, a single bed, and a tall walnut *armoire* (a free standing closet for hanging clothes). She quickly unpacked her possessions and ran downstairs to the first floor to meet the other apprentices—three young Jewish women eager to learn and live in Bad Nauheim. The tall elegant girl with warm brown eyes and jet-black hair was called Hedy. The other two were Paula and Friedel. All of them had arrived today.

They gathered in the light-filled dining room, with its high ceilings outlined by dark brown wood moldings. When she looked out the windows, Hanna could see tables and chairs on a brick lined patio surrounded by green grass and flowering shrubs around the edges of the yard. *These surroundings are part of the cure,* she thought.

Ella explained that food was served buffet style for breakfast, lunch and dinner. The young women would be taught to display foods artistically on platters, arrange flowers for the tables, and set the tables with cutlery, napkins, and glassware. Hanna and the other girls listened attentively as Ella described the meal routine. She then showed the girls how to decorate the foods in the serving dishes with sprigs of lacy green parsley, twists of lemon and orange wheels.

"We'll make the food look as elegant as this beautiful dining room," Hanna exclaimed.

"That's right," answered Ella, her red hair bouncing up and down as she vigorously nodded her head. "We want our guests to enjoy the dining experience with their eyes as well as their mouths."

The girls helped with dining room cleanup after the dinner meal. Ella informed them, "Tonight there is a Mozart concert in the band shell near the bathhouses, and everyone dances in the cafes. Take a walk and enjoy the beautiful weather. The streets will be crowded with people strolling and chatting."

The four of them looked at each other with a mixture of hesitation and eagerness in their eyes. "Let's do it!" exclaimed Paula.

Giggling happily, they hurried upstairs to change clothes and venture forth into the balmy Bad Nauheim dusk

Paula had the map of Bad Nauheim in hand when the four girls, each dressed in softly colored summer frocks, walked from Hotel Weidman to the band shell. The sounds of violins filled the air as the girls sat down on an empty bench to listen to the music. When the concert ended, the four apprentices followed the crowd to the cafes. They stopped at a lively one where a rotund bald man wearing a shiny blue vest was playing Franz Lehar waltzes on his accordion, and people, young and old, were happily dancing. They ordered tea and small iced cakes and sat down to watch. In no time, young men came to the table and asked them to dance. The one who approached Hanna was of medium height and had bright blue eyes and light blonde hair. Hanna thought, *Uh oh, he's probably not Jewish, but we're just dancing, not getting married.* She smiled hesitantly and said, "Yes, I'd like to!"

What fun it was for Hanna to waltz around the small dance floor. Her polka dot dress flared out as she danced round and round. The other girls found dance partners, too. When it was time to walk home, they all talked at once about the music, the boys, and the small amount of guilt they felt about dancing with *goyim* (gentiles).

And so it was that summer. In the evenings at the band shell the orchestra played the music of Bach, Brahms, Mozart, and Beethoven. Sometimes in the afternoons string quartets played next to the beautiful fountain near the ornately decorated bathhouses. And, of course, the girls danced many a night away at the lively cafes. Even though their dance partners wanted to walk them home, the four girls had agreed that they would walk home together.

Their work was easy and, in many ways, creative. They enjoyed decorating the serving dishes of food and had friendly competitions to think up new ways of making the dishes attractive and appetizing. Sometimes they polished the silverware and the silver serving dishes. They picked flowers from the back yard and arranged them in vases.

When the end of spa season approached, Hanna was reluctant to return home to Ulmbach. In a Jewish newspaper, she noticed an ad. It read "WANTED: Companion for elderly woman in Frankfurt. Good salary and ample free time". *Frankfurt!!!! I've always wanted to go there. This may be my chance,* thought Hanna excitedly. She asked Ella Weidman to write her a letter of reference and enclosed it with a quick reply to the ad.

And that's how Hanna became the cook, friend, and helper to Mrs. Bertha Altman. Mrs. Altman lived in a large apartment building near the central gardens. Her spacious apartment was filled with many porcelain figurines, books, and mementos of her life. Thank goodness, there was a separate room for Hanna. The two women, young and old, walked in the gardens, went out for tea or lunch, and sometimes would go to an afternoon opera or concert. Life was much quieter with Mrs. Altman than it had been in Bad Nauheim, but she was able to explore Frankfurt—to go to museums, look in elegant shops, observe beautifully dressed women when they went to the tea gardens. Mrs. Altman loved good books and encouraged Hanna to read them.

Hanna enjoyed her time in the big city, but after three years, she wondered what the next stop on her life journey would be. It was decided for her when Mrs. Altman died, and her mother pleaded with her to return to Ulmbach. Eager to spend time with her mother and her childhood friends, but reluctant to leave the stimulation of a large metropolitan city, she went back home, wondering what her future would hold.

# How Hanna Met
# and Married Joseph

Joseph and Hanna (1939)

Hanna went back to Ulmbach and helped her mother keep the house clean and the garden growing. They canned vegetables and made dill pickles. When the trees bore fruit, it was time to prepare applesauce and sliced pears to can. Hanna visited with her neighbors and read as many books as she could borrow. Time passed slowly.

Hanna longed to be married and have children, but that was not so easy. At that time in Germany, young women needed a substantial dowry to marry well. Hanna's father had died very young in the flu epidemic of 1919, and there wasn't money to provide much of a dowry. And her family lived in a tiny German town where there were no marriageable Jewish men.

Now my mother had a cousin named Rosel. She heard about Joseph living in another tiny town and decided she could do a *mitzvah* (good deed) by introducing Hanna and Joseph with the object of matrimony. She talked to Joseph about Hanna and to Hanna about Joseph. They both seemed interested in meeting. Rosel suggested they write to each other. In his letter, Joseph introduced himself and told my mother he worked as a cattle dealer and could support a wife. He said he would like to be married and have children. He told my mother he had a house in which they could live. My mother wrote back immediately and invited him to visit in Ulmbach when Rosel could be there, too. Joseph traveled three hours by train to see Hanna. They talked about their backgrounds, which were remarkably similar. Both of them had attended school until the eighth grade. Both of them came from religious homes. Both of them were eager to get married. And they were getting on in years. Joseph was thirty-seven years old. Hanna told him she was twenty-nine.

After her death, I found some papers that indicated she was actually thirty-four. What a surprise! Pretending to be younger than you are is a common trick for marriage-hungry women, and Hanna *really* wanted a home of her own and children. Lying about her age probably seemed like a harmless ruse to snare a husband.

Hanna and Joseph saw each other a few times before he proposed. My parents married in 1932 in a small ceremony in Ulmbach. They traveled by train to Nieder-Ohmen to set up housekeeping in the small tan house where I was born the following year. In the evenings after dinner, Papa often strolled to the old family house to see his brother and gossip about business and the doings of the town. For some reason, Mama didn't join him on his outings, maybe because she felt like the outsider in this town where her husband's family was so well known.

My mother brought a little money with her and bought tasteful walnut furniture for the house—a dining table and chairs, a cabinet to hold dishes, and a bedroom set, including an elegant armoire. She was pleased with the furniture, but she wasn't pleased with my father. Perhaps she compared him to her brothers, who were practical men—ambitious and interested in the business world. My father, by contrast, would rather read philosophy than figure out ways to make money. He didn't have an ambitious bone in his body. My mother didn't have a philosophical bone in hers. Their values couldn't have been more different.

My mother never forgave Rosel for introducing her to my father. Whenever Hanna spoke of Cousin Rosel, her voice would develop a hard edge.

Hanna and Joseph didn't have lots of choices. That's a fact. How many Jewish young people lived in tiny German towns? Not very many. Neither Hanna nor Joseph were rich. Being rich would have helped. They would have had more contacts, and she would have had a larger dowry.

My father was idealistic to a fault. My mother was materialistic to a fault. They were like oil and water. It was impossible for them to truly blend. And so they laminated instead of blending. I was a product of the lamination—the only product. Growing up in our house was painful. There was no joking, no laughter, lots of complaining by my mother, lots of sighing, "You know how your mother is" by my father.

I'll give you an example of how opposite they were. After the war, the German government was ordered to make reparations to Jewish people who were forced to leave the country before the war. Since we fled Germany in 1939, the year Hitler invaded Poland, my parents were prime candidates for the program. They had been forced to sell their house for a small fraction of its worth. Hanna asked me to phone for the application to participate in the reparations program. I easily made the call since I was used to being the spokesperson for the Stern family even though I was only eleven years old. When the application arrived, Joseph said, "We have enough. The people rescued from the concentration camps have nothing. We will assign our reparations to them."

From my mother's point of view, the truth was we didn't have very much. Our family lived in a shabby third floor apartment in an old building on Sixteenth Street, a busy Chicago thoroughfare in a low-income area. Both my parents worked very hard, and there was never any money left over for a trip downtown for me to see a first run movie or to buy me a new dress that wasn't on sale in the Sears Roebuck department store catalog. Hanna wanted more things and a more middle class life style.

From my father's point of view, we had a lot. We were alive, living in an apartment with a refrigerator that we bought from Sears, and a gas stove. We had enough to eat, and I was making him proud by being a good student. Most of his family didn't live through the Holocaust. His brother Meier and wife Hedwig, his sister Paula, his sister Toni, his aunt Rifka, and other family members all perished. Only his two nieces, Karola and Hilda, were able to survive Auschwitz.

In German families, the man is the head of the household. Therefore, my father won the battle. Our reparations were assigned to displaced persons who were liberated from the camps. My mother never forgave him.

Many years later, after my father's death, we were having an intimate conversation. She confided that she resented the fact that Papa would go see Uncle Meier in the evenings and didn't stay home with her when I was a baby. I asked her if she thought my father loved her. Her answer was, "He knew from sex. He knew nothing from love." I felt so sorry for them both when she said that.

As an adult woman, I will occasionally be in a doctor's office and pick up a women's magazine that has a column called "Can This Marriage be Saved?" I invariably think of my parents' marriage and say "NO." In today's world, they would have divorced and found people who were better matches for them. In the forties and fifties, they stayed together and made each other miserable.

One day when I was in my thirties, I had taken my mother grocery shopping. I carried the groceries into her apartment, and she invited me to have a cup of coffee. We sat in her kitchen and drank our coffee. She suddenly looked up and said, "You have a lot to be thankful to Hitler for!"

I was shocked and exclaimed, "What in the world do you mean?"

She replied, "If you had stayed in Germany, you would have lived in Nieder-Ohmen. You would have married a small-town man and lived a small-town life. Here you were able to get an education. You wrote a book. You had opportunities you never would have had in Germany. Best of all, you didn't end up like me."

I was heavy-hearted when I heard her poignant words, but I'm certainly glad that my life wasn't a repeat of my mother's. How tragic to work so very hard and yet feel so very frustrated and unfulfilled.

I have experienced my share of sorrow and pain, but I have also felt satisfaction and joy from my relationships with my family and friends and from doing work I find rewarding. I am exceedingly thankful I became "an accidental American."

# What I Learned from My Father

Ruth (standing in rear), Papa Joseph with
Fluffy, Ruth's daughters Felicia and Amy
with Goldie

My father, Joseph Stern, felt like a country bumpkin in Chicago—having spent the first forty-five years of his life being a cattle dealer in Nieder-Ohmen, a town of fourteen hundred, in rural Germany. He knew everyone there, and everyone knew him.

The Stern family is listed in the town records as early as 1753. In her book, *Words that Burn Within Me,* my cousin, Hilda Stern Cohen, writes, "I don't know how long Jews have lived there, but I think they came with the Romans. Until the end of the eighteenth century, they were the semi-serfs of local feudal lords. Lacking the right to permanent residency, they were forced to move from one village to another. Then they were given permission to settle permanently." My grandfather's house had a wooden beam across the main door with *1558* carved into it. His father, Abraham, had purchased the home. Abraham Stern, my great-grandfather, was the first person to be buried in the new Jewish cemetery.

My paternal grandmother's family name was Andorn. I was told that it originated in the tiny country of Andorra, nestled in the mountains between Spain and France. Remembering that Andorra was a strongly Catholic country and that the Spanish Inquisition was still going strong in the late fourteen hundreds, it's easy to figure out why they left and looked for a more hospitable place to settle. For some reason they picked a village in central Germany, one that was close enough to Nieder-Ohmen so that my grandfather, Hirsch, met and married Roschen. Hilda writes about "an annual Purim ball in the springtime during which young people from other villages were introduced to each other for the purpose of marriage." Perhaps that's how they met.

In rural Germany, many Jewish men were cattle dealers, which was a service useful to local farmers. The Stern family, for at least three generations, had been cattle dealers. By the time Joseph was born in 1894, the family was very much part of the ongoing commercial life in Nieder-Ohmen. My father and his brother, Meier, went into the family business.

My father only studied through the eighth grade in school. But that didn't stop him from reading Goethe, Heine, and Schiller—famous German philosophers. When he was a boy, he also read James Fenimore Cooper's books about the American wilderness and dreamed about "the wide open spaces."

I learned about the pleasures of reading from Papa. He not only liked to read, but he liked to tell me what he was reading, and I was a good listener, even when I didn't know what he was talking about. He said, "Reading is a way to learn about the world and about the different ways people look at life." As a child, I remember loving books that told stories about faraway places, and I still do.

In 1914 at the start of World War I, Uncle Meier was twenty-three years old and Joseph was nineteen. They both fought honorably for the German Fatherland. My father was captured by the Russians in Bulgaria and spent six months in a prison camp. Papa said the Russians treated him well, and he relished the chance to talk to the guards and find out about their country and philosophy. For the rest of his life, he was sympathetic to socialistic ideals. He brought back coins from Austria, Hungary, and Bulgaria that I loved to play with. Now I have mounted them on velvet, and they hang on my living room wall.

Until Papa married Mama, he lived in the sprawling ancestral Stern home with his father, who died in 1930, his brother and sister-in-law, Meier and Hedwig, their two young daughters, Hilda and Karola, and his sister, Toni. His social life revolved around his brother's family, and he had many good friends among the farmers of the community. These were men he had known his whole life. They had gone to school together, played games together, and exchanged books to read. There was a high level of trust between them.

The synagogue in Nieder-Ohmen was a house that had been remodeled. There were never more than thirty Jewish families in the town. The Jewish people observed Sabbath on Saturday. In the morning, we would go to services. On Saturday afternoon, everyone would go for a walk. There were many activities forbidden on the Sabbath, but walking and visiting with friends were encouraged. My father was a strong walker with a long stride. I had to run to keep up with him.

Try to imagine how life was for Joseph in those early days in Chicago. He felt like a little fish, crowded by big fish, in a large unfamiliar lake. The hustle and bustle of big city life bewildered him. Everyone seemed to be scurrying about, going in different directions. Streetcars, buses, trucks and cars sped down the busy streets. He couldn't speak the language or understand the signs. He so missed the gentle rolling hills and peaceful surroundings of his beloved Nieder-Ohmen. Yet, he knew that being free in Chicago was better than being oppressed in Nieder-Ohmen. Like many immigrants before him, he thought, *this may be the hardest thing I ever have to do, but I will find work and adjust to life in Chicago.*

From 1940 to 1945, my father was obsessed with following the progress of the Allied forces fighting the war against Nazi Germany. Each evening he poured over maps in the newspapers to see where the troops were fighting. I learned a lot about the location of the European countries during those years. Perhaps my desire to visit all those countries came from seeing map after map of them.

Papa never found work that interested him in Chicago. His first job was pulling the feathers from dead chickens in a butcher shop. That was the only work he could find in 1939. He did that for few months until he landed a job as a beef boner in the stockyards. Ironically, he went from dealing with live cattle to cutting up dead ones. He much preferred live ones.

My dad really liked cattle. Many years later, when he moved to Livermore California, he would sometimes ride his bike out to the fields on North Livermore Avenue and stroke the heads of the cattle that would come to see him as he stood by the fence.

His favorite American tune became *"Don't Fence Me In"*. "Oh give me land, lots of land under starry skies above. Don't fence me in. Let me ride in the wide-open country that I love. Don't fence me in." I am sure the song reflected his regret at 'being fenced in'—living in a crowded city when he wished he were living a rural life "with starry skies above."

My dad was also attracted to the Irish music of the time—"Danny Boy", "I'll Take You Home Again, Kathleen"—sad songs that, no doubt, reflected his frequent longing to be somewhere else.

On Saturday afternoons in Chicago my father and I would go for the traditional Nieder-Ohmen Sabbath walk. Douglas Park was close to our house. It was a typical big city park—mowed weedy grass with tall old maple and oak trees scattered everywhere. There was a lagoon in the center, and we would often walk on the asphalt path around the lagoon, pointing out the ducks and geese serenely swimming along its edge. Frequently we walked without my mother, who liked a peaceful Saturday nap. Spending time alone with my father was a treat, and I learned to become a fast walker to keep up with his long strides. At least now I no longer had to run. To this day, people comment on how rapidly I walk. It's something else I learned from my father.

Politics was a frequent topic of discussion at our house during those turbulent days of World War II. My father was a great admirer of President Franklin Delano Roosevelt. Papa found a photo of him on the cover of the Sunday newspaper magazine, very carefully cut it out, and framed it. I remember it hanging for years on the wall right above the radiator in the living room. I have always been interested in the political process and what I can do to make even a small impact. I credit my father's influence with that.

Papa was a man of his generation. He could talk about a book he read, or a battle that the U.S. Army won, but he never discussed his fears, his tender feelings, or his frustrations. "Real men" didn't talk about such things to his way of thinking. My father told me, "Actions speak louder than words. Look at the way General George Marshall acted to keep Europe from starving after World War II by starting the Marshall Plan. That's real action to make the world a better place."

Dad didn't just look up to people who were acting to make the world a better place. In his own small and very personal way, he acted, too. We never owned a car. Our family rode public transit daily. My father noticed that whenever a Black person was sitting next to the window, white people would not sit next to them. Papa realized this was due to the racist attitudes existing at the time. So, he made it his mission to sit next to Blacks whenever he rode public transit. Seeing him do that as a child, I learned to follow his example, and I always felt pleased when I could make this small gesture of good will.

Years later, I asked him about it. He thoughtfully replied, "I know first hand what it feels like to be discriminated against. I don't like to see it happening here. I decided to show myself and the other people on the bus that I don't discriminate against Blacks. Sometimes I saw another rider sit next to a Black person after I did, and I felt happy."

I have often wished my father's life had been happier, but when I realize that seeing someone else follow his example made him happy, I think perhaps he had more happy moments than I knew.

# Being Three
# and Bewildered

Three Year Old Ruth and Oma Fannie

(1936)

Being a little girl in a village of 1,400 people in rural Germany felt safe and friendly to me in the 1930's. Even at the age of three, I could tell my mother that I was going to see Anna, and walk to her house. I'd help Anna shell peas or make cookies. Everyone in the neighborhood knew me, and I knew them. Often in the evening after dinner my father and I walked to my Uncle Meier's house. The two brothers would talk worriedly about what was happening in their country while my cousin, Karola, and I would play. Even though she was eight years older than I, she always thought up games to play with me.

Everything changed the first night I heard the sound of loud martial music sung by adolescent boys accented by the accompaniment of their boots stomping on the cobblestones outside. My parents turned out the lights in the house, stood in a corner of the dining room and furtively looked out through the sheer window curtains to watch the *Hitler Jugend* (Hitler Youth) marching down our street. The boys had rocks in their hands. Whenever they saw the lights on in a Jewish home, they threw rocks at the house.

I didn't understand what was happening. I just knew that my mother was frightened and even my usually calm father was uneasy. So, I was confused and scared. Several times a week, whenever the Hitler Youth had an evening meeting, the scenario was repeated. If we forgot to turn off the lights, the sound of the rocks as they smashed into the house was "thud! thud!" They aimed for the windows, but they never hit their target.

Everything seemed different now. Our neighbors were not as friendly—at least, not when other people might see them. There were Nazi spies everywhere who would report Germans who "fraternized with the Jews." The relaxed, comfortable feeling I had when I left our house was no longer there. The tension in our little town affected everyone—grownups and children alike. Life in Nieder-Ohmen would never be the same.

# Tante Rifka

Tante Rifka (1937)

*Tante* Rifka was my father's aunt and my mother's nemesis. She came with our house like the wood stove and the water pump in the sink. Here's the story I was told. Grandfather Hirsch owned two houses in Nieder-Ohmen, the small German town where I was born. One was the old sprawling family house built of mud and sticks in the 1500's. The other was considerably smaller and newer—a modest two story tan bungalow with a steep roof so that the winter snows would slide off. When my grandfather died, he left the family home to his eldest son, Meier, and the bungalow to my father, Joseph.

While Papa was a bachelor, he lived in the family home with his brother's family. They included Aunt Hedwig, my cousins, Hilda and Karola, and my aunt Toni. Everyone said Toni was "slow". Mama explained, "Her brain didn't grow while her body did. Her body is that of a grown-up woman, but she has the brain of an eight-year-old." I liked Aunt Toni. She and I would find shiny black beetles in the dirt and watch them until they crawled back into the rich brown garden soil.

Now for a small-town Jewish man to find a wife was complicated since there were often only two or three Jewish families in the whole community. Frequently, a friend or relative knew of an eligible partner and did a little informal matchmaking. Mama's cousin Rosel introduced her to Papa, and they decided to get married.

Papa went to work fixing up the little tan bungalow. He scraped off old peeling paint. He painted the inside with soft pastel colors. He sanded the well-worn oak floorboards. But he couldn't fix up *Tante* Rifka. She lived in the small apartment on the second floor, and she was there to stay, no matter who else lived in the house.

*Tante* Rifka was a square woman. Her simple floral house dresses hung from her shoulders to well below her knees, but not to the ground. I remember she wore heavy black work shoes with white stockings. Her wispy gray hair was parted in the middle and twisted into a no-nonsense bun at the back of her head. Her face had lots of frown lines on it—a down turned mouth with thin disapproving lips, and deep furrows between her eyes.

When I think about it now, I realize *Tante* Rifka was simply unhappy and bitter. After all, life had passed her by. She had no husband to keep her company. She had no children to care for her in her old age. She had no grandchildren to carry on her genes. At the time, she seemed mean and vindictive, especially to my mother—the "other woman" who had invaded her territory.

"Thump!" "Thump!" "Thump!" About five o'clock in the morning *Tante* Rifka would stomp on the upstairs floor. We'd hear her shout, "Joseph! I'm cold. Get yourself out of bed and put wood into the heater." My father would holler back, "Go to back to bed, *Tante* Rifka, and stay warm. The sun is still asleep. You should be, too!"

Most of her ire was directed at Mama. *Tante* Rifka complained to her, "Stop cooking cabbage. The odor is too strong. I can smell the stench upstairs." "I wanted to wash clothes today, and you've used up the entire clothesline." "That child of yours is making too much noise. Keep her quiet!" Whenever she was annoyed, we heard "thump!" "thump!" "thump!" as she expressed her anger with her feet.

Once in awhile Aunt Toni came to see her. Aunt Toni was unaware of all the bitterness in the house. She liked Aunt Rifka, and she liked me. "Come upstairs with me to see Aunt Rifka," she pleaded. "She'll give us cake." My mother nodded that it was fine with her.

I ran up the stairs, and Toni climbed slowly behind me. At the top, I waited for Toni to knock. *Tante* Rifka answered the door, and there was a smile on her face. "Come in! Come in!"

She beamed. "I made a cake just for my company." I was amazed. *Cake? Smiles? Company? What was going on?* As I sat down on the couch and devoured my raisin-filled cake, I watched *Tante* Rifka. She had a small red ball and a beat up old metal mixing bowl. "Look!" she called. "Let's see who can get the ball in the bowl." As Toni and I laughed and played, *Tante* Rifka's face softened and her eyes shown. Somehow I realized that *Tante* Rifka's was getting what she most wanted—company and attention.

# A *Sunday Morning* Encounter

The spacious two-story farmhouse was set in the center of the U-shaped cobblestone courtyard. The animals lived on the left side in the barn, and their feed was stored on the right side in the shed. Although it was still early in the day, about nine o'clock, warm July sunlight caressed the small cluster of houses that was Nieder-Ohmen.

The house in the courtyard was one of the largest in the village. It belonged to the Ohnacker family, who were hard working and prosperous farmers. Our family's house, unpretentious and perhaps even a bit shabby, stood next door.

On this particular Sunday morning, Frau Ohnacker was in the courtyard busily at work, her light gray summer frock covered by a severe dark blue apron. She was a sturdy peasant woman of about 50—of medium height, with broad shoulders. If you saw her, you would have known instantly that she was in charge of her household, and that she was a warm-hearted, kind woman, who exuded friendly confidence. I saw her from our porch and ran up to her with four-year-old bounciness. I was wearing a pink and blue flowered cotton dress that blew around my legs as I ran over the uneven cobblestones. My short dark hair framed a small heart-shaped face in which tea colored brown eyes sparkled with friendly curiosity.

"Frau Ohnacker, what are you doing?" I asked.

"We are going to church in a little while, and I am polishing my husband's shoes," she replied.

"Frau Ohnacker, is there something wrong with your husband? Why can't he polish his own shoes?"

Many years later, in 1979, my two daughters, my husband, and I visited Nieder-Ohmen. The neighbors I remembered from my childhood were all still living there. They decided to have an impromptu party to celebrate our return. Hearty German foods appeared as if by magic—lots of sausages, dark breads, apple strudel, and fruit tarts. Neighbors told stories about my family to entertain my husband Burt and my daughters Amy, 18, and Felicia, 14.

Frau Ohnacker, still strong and alert in her 80's, told us she never forgot the day I wondered why her husband didn't polish his own shoes. Of course, she would never have suggested anything so radical to her husband, but she had told the story through the years to family and friends.

When my husband heard it, he threw back his head and laughed heartily. "Ruth," he chuckled, "you must have been Germany's first 'women's libber' in 1938 at the age of four. Even then you were sticking up for oppressed minorities, and you haven't changed a bit!"

# Sled Riding in the Moonlight

A soft, gentle snow had fallen on Nieder-Ohmen during the day. The little village looked like a winter painting with its steeply roofed timbered houses covered in their blankets of white nestled in gently rolling hills.

The time was six in the evening. Darkness had fallen. You could see lights in houses and hear sounds of meat and potatoes sizzling in pans as the farmers' wives prepared meals. The men had finished their chores and were washing up before dinner.

My mother, my father, and I had just sat down to dinner. The adults with tense faces talked in hushed tones about "Crystal Night."

"What's "Crystal Night?" I asked.

Mama angrily replied, "The Nieder-Ohmen Nazis destroyed our little synagogue!"

"Why do you call it "Crystal Night?" I persisted.

"Because everywhere in Germany, the windows of Jewish businesses and synagogues were broken. The streets were strewn with shards of glass. It was a very bad thing to do, and it was done by some very bad people who blame others for their problems," answered Mama.

"The decent German people will not put up with this behavior by hooligans. They will rise up and put a stop to it," Papa said reassuringly.

"Don't count on it!" snapped my mother. No one said anything. I stabbed the peas with my fork and put them in my mouth.

"Knock, Knock." A lilting voice was heard at the door. "It's me, Anna. I have my sled, and I'm looking for a playmate. Can Ruthie come sledding with me?"

I jumped up from the table and flung open the door. Anna was dressed in a wooly blue tweed jacket, a knit white cap and warm black mittens. Thick black stockings covered her legs, and she wore sturdy work shoes, as did most of the farm wives of the 1930's. Anna's friendly smile and sparkly blue eyes brought instant relief from the tension of the dinner table conversation.

"Oh, please, Mama! May I go with Anna?"

"Yes, you may," my mother answered quickly. "I'll get your jacket and warm leggings, we'll dress you for the cold night."

I was so excited that I jumped up and down. Going sledding with Anna was one of my favorite things to do. Anna lived next door and didn't have any children of her own. She was a lively young woman who just loved being with children, and she was naturally gifted at it. If she were alive today, she'd probably be a pre-school teacher.

Last year Anna and I went sledding in the afternoons after Anna finished her chores. This year we went sledding in the evenings. I thought that evening sledding was even more fun than afternoon sledding. It was somehow slightly mysterious to be on the hill behind the houses in the dark.

It was just as well as well that I didn't know the reason for the time change in our schedule, but Anna did, and so did my mother and father. All three of them knew that Anna was taking a risk to be "fraternizing with the Jews." In the evening there was less chance of being seen by the Hitler Youth and being reported to the authorities. No one spoke of this. There were murmured words of greeting by the three adults as Mama put on my warm maroon coat with its matching leggings and hat. She then wrapped a white scarf around my neck and shoved my hands into green mittens. I thought *I'm so warmly dressed that I could go where the polar bears live.*

I grabbed Anna's hand and pulled her to the door as soon as Mama released me. The wooden sled was standing in front of the house. Anna took one side of the rope. I picked up the other. Together we pulled the sled up the gently sloping hill. Anna was singing a silly song about the boy who lost his shoe in Lauterbach and couldn't go home without it. I joined in, and the two of us laughingly trudged up the snowy hill. When we got to the top, Anna climbed on the sled and tucked me in front of her, with her strong arms encircling me ever so securely. Anna pushed off, and we smoothly glided down the hill and came to a gentle stop at the bottom.

A full moon had risen. As again and again we pulled the sled to the top of the hill and slid down, the moon caressed us, and we saw our shadows on snow that sparkled in the moonlight. It must have been over an hour later when Anna said, "The cow will want to be milked early in the morning. It's time to go home."

I reluctantly returned to the tense little house in Nieder-Ohmen, but for one evening in the moonlight—all was right with the world.

# The Trip to Stuttgart

German Soldiers Marching in Nieder-Ohmen (1933)

We got off the train at the main station in Stuttgart. If you had been there, you would have seen my mother, a slim woman in her late thirties, wearing a slate gray coat, a snug fitting black wool hat, sensible black walking shoes and carrying a rather large black leather handbag. She was not tall—only about 5 feet 2 inches, but there was strength and determination about her. Her brown curly hair kept trying to escape from her hat in tiny wisps here and there. Her gray eyes looked worried, and there was a frown on her forehead. She stepped down from the train first and then lifted me, a little five-year-old girl, off the high step.

I was dressed in a different fashion from my mother. I was wearing a smart maroon wool coat and matching bonnet, which tied under my chin. As I walked, you could catch glimpses of the pink cotton dress I wore—my very best dress. I carried a pink print bag with little flowers on it—most definitely homemade. Peering out from the bag was a rag doll, and there seemed to be a small book or two in the bottom of it. I could have been going to a birthday party or to visit my grandmother. The expression in my brown eyes was a combination of excitement at being in such a large bustling city and fear because I had been infected by my mother's apprehension.

My mother took me firmly by the hand and walked quickly to the ticket booth. "Excuse me," she said to the agent, "Could you please tell me how to get to SS Headquarters?" (The SS were the highly feared special military that ran the "work camps.")

"Yes, madam. Walk on this street for one half kilometer and turn right at Hamburg Street. The headquarters are the fourth building on the left side of the street."

"Thank you for your help," whispered Mama, managing a wan smile.

And so my mother and I walked down the street in Stuttgart under a gray winter sky. We saw warmly dressed women doing their daily marketing, carrying loaves of bread and bags of carrots and potatoes. It was early in December, and some holiday decorations could be seen in stores as we passed. From somewhere close by "*Oh Tannenbaum*" was playing on a radio. I was entranced by the store windows. The first store we passed had dishes of many different designs on display—some with gold borders, others with brightly painted flowers. There were shiny copper pots and sturdy black frying pans, delicate goblets with designs etched in their sides and elegant pitchers to match. The next store sold linens—soft feather comforters, embroidered pillowcases and sheets, and lovely tablecloths—all tastefully arranged in the show window. Best of all was the toy store. With Christmas so near, the window was bursting with brightly colored playthings—dolls of all sizes, train sets made of wood and metal, puppets, and animal wind-up toys. There were puzzles and books, too.

"Oh, please, Mama, can't we go in for just a minute?" I pleaded.

"Now, Ruthie, you know we have a 10:30 appointment. There is no time to go to a store now," her mother answered tersely. She took my hand firmly and walked rapidly onward.

We finally arrived at the imposing three-story brick building. There was a uniformed guard on each side of the large carved wooden double door. As we walked up the three steps to the entrance, my mother straightened her back, took a deep breath, and then pushed open the door. The two of us hesitantly stepped into the imposing hallway. There was a small crystal chandelier hanging from the carved ceiling, and the colored mosaic tiles on the floor were in a swirled design. Perhaps this building had been the home of some rich German industrialist's family long ago. It was certainly elegant enough.

In the center of the hallway, there was a simple wooden desk with a uniformed young man seated behind it. My mother and I approached him. "My name is Hanna Stern. I have an appointment with the commandant at 10:30".

"Please be seated. He will see you shortly," replied the young man politely. We sat down next to each other. I stroked the yellow yarn hair on my rag doll, which was wearing a pink dress, too. In fact, my mother had sewed the doll's dress from fabric scraps left over from my dress.

"Commandant Messer is ready for you," announced the man at the desk. "This way, please." He ushered my mother and me into a large wood paneled office with a high ceiling and an Oriental rug on the floor. Sitting at a huge desk was an ordinary looking middle-aged man in a well-tailored dark uniform. His straw colored hair was thinning, and his blue eyes were framed by wire-rimmed spectacles.

He looked up from his papers as the two of us walked in and said sharply, "You asked to see me. What do you want?"

Standing very close to my mother, I could hear her take a deep breath. Mama held on to my wrist so tightly that it hurt, but I didn't make a sound. After what seemed like a long pause, Mama said, "I have come to ask for the release of Joseph Stern, my husband, from Buchenwald, the work camp to which the Jewish men from Nieder-Ohmen were sent. You see, my family in America has sent papers for us to go there. I received them just last week after Joseph was already gone. If he is released, we will sell our belongings and leave as soon as possible."

The man behind the desk was silent for a moment. Then he turned to me and said, "I have a daughter, too. She's six, and her name is Trudie. What's your name, and how old are you?"

I replied in a quiet, frightened voice, "Ruth. I'm five. My doll is Heidi. She's two."

Commandant Messer turned to Mama and stated, "I will sign the papers to have your husband released. He will be home within a week."

I felt Mama's fingers around my wrist relax as she exclaimed with great joy, "Oh, thank you! Thank you, Herr Commandant. You are a kind man."

Commandant Messer looked down at his papers and seemed momentarily touched by Mama's relief and gratitude. He cleared his throat. Then he ordered brusquely, "On your way out, send my assistant in, and I'll get the necessary paper work done."

Mama knew it was time to leave, and she gently took my hand and left the spacious office. We stopped in the reception room to tell the young man that the commandant wished to see him and then quickly left the building—almost as if Mama were afraid that Commandant Messer might change his mind if we tarried.

What a different mood! Mama smiled and gaily chatted with me. She even allowed me to run ahead. "I have an idea!" exclaimed Mama. "Let's stop at a café and have cocoa and cake. And then it's off to the toy store to buy you a plaything to take to America. We have a whole new life awaiting us."

# My Pal, Rosie

"Papa, Papa, can we take a walk to the field and visit Rosie?" I shouted to my father as I bounded into the living room. I was wearing a flower print cotton dress—small pastel flowers on a light blue background. It was a proper dress for a little girl to wear on the Sabbath in the mid-thirties in small town Germany. On Saturday, the Sabbath, work was forbidden. You were not supposed to make fires, write, carry money, or turn on lights. There were lots of things you shouldn't do, but going for a walk was permissible.

My father was lying on the dark green velvet couch—totally immersed in a book that he held in front of his face. He looked up, smiled at me and said, "Just let me finish this chapter, and I'll go with you."

My father was reading about the American wilderness—a novel written by James Fennimore Cooper. He loved reading about wide-open spaces, cowboys, and their adventures.

The sun shone on the two of us as we walked the path the cows took when they went to pasture. The September sun warmed our backs, but the clear autumn air held a warning of winter to come. "Crunch, crunch, crunch!" Our feet stepped on dried grasses, creating a pleasant noise as we walked along briskly. I took three or four steps for each of my father's long easy strides. He held my hand, and we talked about my Uncle Meier, my Aunt Hedwig, and my two girl cousins, Hilda and Karola, who were ten and eight years older than I.

I carried some wilted spinach to give Rosie when we arrived at the pasture. As soon as Rosie saw us, she mooed and came over. Papa and I both stroked her and told her what a good cow she was. She stood still and relished the attention she was getting. Rosie's coat was a rich reddish brown color; and in the middle of her face, there was a white diamond. I thought she was the most beautiful cow in the whole world.

Every afternoon when Rosie walked back to her stall with all the other village cows, I would run down the front stairs of our house and dash into her stall, which was underneath and to one side of the house—like a garage might be. Our house was located on a small hill, and Rosie's stall fit perfectly. My father's milking stool was right there. He used it every morning and evening to milk Rosie and bring up the sweet, warm milk for me to drink. I climbed on the stool and shared the events of the day with Rosie.

"Today I went to see Hilda and Karola. We had a tea party, and Aunt Hedwig made us some sugar cookies to eat. I like Karola better than Hilda because she laughs a lot and plays with me more."

Sometimes Rosie would lick my hand with her long red sandpapery tongue. Once in awhile she'd lick the top of my head. When she did that, I would giggle.

When the people in the village wouldn't look at us at the store, I told Rosie about it. When the Hitler Youth threw stones at our house and yelled "Dirty Jews!" Rosie was the first to find out about my confusion.

The day that the SS took my father away to Buchenwald, which was called a "Work Camp", Herr Ohnacker, our neighbor, knocked on our door and quietly said to my mother, "I am sorry about Joseph. I will milk Rosie for you." My mother and I were grateful, especially me. I loved drinking the sweet, warm milk every morning and evening. I felt like the milk was Rosie's gift just for me.

I missed my father a lot. In the afternoons, Rosie looked at me with her soft brown eyes and seemed to sense my sadness and fear about all the bad things that were happening to my family. "Oh, Rosie! Mamma is so quiet. Her face looks sad and worried. I'm worried, too. I hope Papa's okay."

I hugged Rosie and cried softly.

"Rosie! Rosie! Papa's coming home. Mama and I made it happen. We went to Stuttgart and talked to the SS Commandant. He said he has a little girl my age, and he's going to let Papa come home! Aren't you happy, Rosie?" Rosie licked the top of my head. I gave her some lettuce to eat and hugged her very hard.

When Papa came home, Mama told him she had written to her cousins in America and asked them to sponsor us to immigrate to the United States and that she had received the proper papers from them. Papa stroked his chin thoughtfully and said with a sigh, "Yes, we must leave. There is no future for us here. The good people are afraid, and the Nazis have all the power."

Mama and Papa were running here, there, and everywhere to get ready to leave Germany. So much to do. They didn't have any time for me. Every afternoon

Rosie heard about the preparations. Mama went to Frankfurt and bought new sheets, pillowcases, warm wool blankets, soft fluffy towels, beautiful embroidered tablecloths and napkins. Then she washed everything. I thought that was a strange thing to do. Why wash brand new things? Mama explained that people who were leaving Germany were not supposed to take new items with them. Washing the linens made them look used.

One day, I slowly walked into Rosie's stall and stroked her side. I wonder if she noticed I had been crying. "Rosie, Herr Schmidt is buying our house. He's going to buy you, too. You'll be able to stay right here in your cozy stall, go to the pasture with your friends just like always. I wish you could go with us. Papa says we're going to a big city called Chicago, and nobody has cows there. When we're in America, I hope you'll remember me. You're my best friend, and I'll never forget you."

# *Cousin Hilda is Famous*

The Original Stern Family Home
(photo around 1910-1920)

When I was born in Nieder-Ohmen, Germany, in 1933, cousin Hilda was ten years old, a thin, serious girl with dark straight hair and large brown eyes. She lived in the old Stern family home just a few blocks away with her mother, Aunt Hedwig, her father, Uncle Meier, Papa's older brother, and her lively younger sister, Karola, who was eight years old. Papa and I walked to their house to see them many evenings while Mama cleaned up the dishes after dinner.

Sometimes I brought my doll, Heidi, along. Karola and I would play house and talk to each other. She told me about her friends at school and asked me questions about my day. I remember Hilda sitting near a lamp and reading books. She didn't pay attention to me, and I thought that she must be really smart because she read so much. Her father, Uncle Meier complained to Papa, "Nothing will come of Hilda. All she wants to do is read."

In 1935, Karola and Hilda were no longer allowed to go to school in Nieder-Ohmen because we were Jewish. Karola was terribly hurt when her best friend, Alma, told her that she couldn't play with Karola anymore. She explained, "My mother won't let me play with Jews."

Uncle Meier made arrangements for his daughters to go to Jewish schools away from home. Hilda went first to Frankfurt, lived with my Aunt Paula and Uncle Nathan, and studied at a Jewish day school. After a year, she was offered a chance to go to the Training Seminary for

Jewish Teachers in Wurzburg. Karola went to a school for boys and girls in Bad Nauheim. Little did she know that she'd meet her future husband at that school. But that's another story.

I was too young to go to school, and I missed having them around in the evenings. Now Papa and Uncle Meier sat close together and talked quietly and seriously about what Hitler was doing to create hatred against us in the town where our family had lived for hundreds of years.

"Don't worry, Joseph," Uncle Meier reassured Papa. "The German people won't put up with Hitler's nonsense for long. Wait and see! They'll vote him out of power." Papa shook his head and said in a worried voice, "I'd like to believe that, but I see no hopeful signs. Good German people here are afraid that they will be turned in as Jewish sympathizers by their neighbors. Others just don't want to get involved. Still others want to get rid of us. They buy Hitler's propaganda."

Mama was sure the Jews were in for terrible torments and didn't want to wait and see what would happen. She wrote to her father's sister in Chicago, USA.

*"Dear Aunt Dina,*

*Life is hard for us in Germany. The government wants the Jews out of the country. We need to leave. We hope you will sponsor us. We will work hard in the USA and will be no trouble for you and your family. I hope to hear from you soon.*

*Your niece,*

*Hannah"*

A few days after *Kristallnach* (November 9, 1938—the night that synagogues, Jewish businesses and homes were vandalized, looted and burned across Germany) my father was taken to Buchenwald, then called a "work camp." Mama received the sponsorship papers from Aunt Dina two days later. Her reaction was a mixture of great relief and great confusion. Now that her husband was imprisoned in Buchenwald, what could she do to get him released so that we could leave this frightening place? Her solution to the problem is the subject of an earlier chapter. The upshot of it was that Mama, Papa and I left Germany on a huge ocean liner and sailed to America.

Uncle Meier's family remained in Germany. As life for the Jewish people became more and more difficult, the Bad Nauheim school was closed by the Nazis. Karola and some of her classmates were sent to Berlin to work in a German military factory. Eventually, she was deported to Auchschwitz, in Poland, a concentration camp where the extermination of Jews, Gypsies, homosexuals, and developmentally disabled people was routinely carried out. Karola was a teenager—strong and street smart. Miraculously, she survived her internment in the camp. She was put to work as a person who shaved the heads of new arrivals.

She knew that her parents and her sister, Hilda, had been sent to the ghetto in Lodz, Poland. Karola heard that cattle cars carrying Jews from the Lodz ghetto were expected at Auchschwitz. With great courage, she approached the camp director and asked if she could go to the ramp with him the to see if her parents and sister were among the new arrivals. He answered, "I won't let a girl go to the trains, but if you find a man to go and call their names, he may try."

Karola had many friends; so finding a young man to go to the trains was easy. She asked Bumeck if he would go. "Of course, I will," he quickly consented. At the place where the cattle cars were being unloaded, he called, "Meier Stern! Hedwig Stern!" Many people cried out that they were Hedwig and Meier, but when he asked them what their children's names were, nobody said "Karola and Hilda." He went back and gave Karola the bad news.

Karola didn't know that both her parents had died in the Lodz ghetto. Hilda did go to the Auschwitz on the transports. She was put in the line that was going to be sent to the camp—not in the line that was immediately sent to the gas chambers. As part of being processed into Auschwitz, everyone's head was shaved. Hilda recognized Karola as one of the girls doing that job. The two sisters had a tearful reunion. Even the SS supervisor was touched and said that Karola would not have to shave Hilda's head, just cut her hair short.

Karola had been at the camp for about two years. She managed to get a little bread and sugar for her starving sister. Karola looked after Hilda and tried to help her gain some strength. This was not easy when there was never enough to eat. When the SS guards heard that the Russians were coming, they marched the prisoners away from the camp. Karola and Hilda escaped from the group and hid in the woods until they were found by some Russian soldiers who gave them food and helped them.

Finally, the two girls made their way to Austria where they lived in a camp for refugees until we and other family members were able to bring them to the United States. So many refugees and so much red tape. The arrangements took about a year. Hilda hadn't changed. In the refugee camp, she found books to read, and Karola saw her writing in a notebook. She never showed her writing to anyone—not even her sister.

Hilda and Karola did come to the United States. Hilda met and married Werner, a graduate student in chemistry, who was German and who had been in England during the war. He had lost his parents and understood the horrors of the Holocaust. They had three daughters and settled in Baltimore. Hilda lived a long and productive life, teaching Hebrew and being a respected member of the Jewish community.

Sadly, she died a few years ago. When Werner was going through some of her papers, he found German poetry and stories that she had written during that year in Austria. He read them with amazement. *This is extremely good poetry,* he thought and showed it to a German professor. The professor was impressed and declared, "Werner, these poems should be published. I know a publisher in Germany. I suggest you take them to him and see what he says."

What a response Werner received! "These poems are as good as those by Heinrich Heine," the publisher told him. "We will be honored to publish them."

Her poems and stories are being read by thousands of German school children. The book has now been translated into English under the title *Words That Burn Within Me.*

I am happy to report that my cousin Hilda amounted to something after all, even though all she wanted to do was read books. Cousin Hilda is famous!

# Leaving for America

The *S.S. Deutschland*

"Hamburg! Hamburg! This the final stop of this train. Everybody off!" the conductor shouted. Along with hundreds of other passengers in their muted winter coats, hats and scarves, my father in his bulky brown overcoat and my mother in her dark blue one disembarked into the train station. Papa was carrying two large suitcases and Mama two smaller ones. Papa set his down on the platform, turned to the train and lifted me off the top step. I, too, was wearing a warm coat to ward off the January chill. Mine was maroon and flared out at the waist. Mama had bought it in Giessen, and I thought it was ever so pretty

I was sleepy and disoriented. My mother had packed lots of food for the nine-hour trip from Nieder-Ohmen to Hamburg, the seaport where we were to board the ship that would sail to America. Some dark bread, yellow cheese, and a shiny red apple helped me to regain some of my five-year-old interest in everything that was happening around me.

I looked at my father in his brown hat, brown shoes, and brown coat with his brown eyes. Suddenly, he looked like a brown bear that I remembered from my animal picture book. My mother had a narrow face and a prominent nose. Around her neck she wore a light blue scarf that went nicely with her navy blue coat. She reminded me of a fragile blue shore bird. Yes, the food was working. My imagination had returned.

Along with other suitcase-laden passengers, we were herded on to buses bound for the ship dock. All of us were Germans who were fleeing because of Hitler's persecutions. There were people who openly disagreed with the regime—professors, writers, homosexuals, and, of course, Jews.

The bus stopped at an enormous square building that must have been a warehouse once. As I remember the building, it was slate gray, the same color as the sky that blustery January morning. Inside there were so many blue uniformed men and women scurrying about, it reminded me of the ant hills that I liked to watch in the pasture near our house. I looked around the building, and I could see the large metal braces that held up the roof. The floor was gray concrete. There were tables set up in long rows with uniformed men behind them and departing refugees slowly moving in front of them. The officials were using harsh, commanding voices to direct the would-be ship passengers here and there. "Stand in this line!" "Put your suitcase on the table!" Their voices bounced off the hard, empty walls, and there was an unpleasant din. While the administrators were loud and officious, the endless line of people in front of the long tables spoke quietly in respectful and sometimes hesitant tones.

The building had been turned into a center for examining the luggage and bodies of the departing refugees to make sure they didn't take anything valuable out of the country. I remember the experience as being humiliating. I can only imagine how it was for my parents.

My mother and I were directed to an area for women on the left side of the cavernous room. There the uniformed officials were women. After we went through the gauntlet and had put on our clothes again, we were told to exit by the door in front of us. All at once, it was over. We were outside in the cold fresh air. Papa rushed up and exclaimed, "Oh, I am glad to see you. I wondered where you were."

Now there were new sounds—a man playing Strauss waltzes on an accordion, people chatting, sounds of tears and sounds of laughter.

I looked straight ahead and saw a huge ship. It looked like it was big enough to hold all the people from Nieder-Ohmen and from Giessen, too. I had never seen anything so massive in my life. It had three red smoke stacks, and there were clouds of white smoke coming from each of them. Papa told me it was called the *S.S. Deutschland.* There were already people on the ship. Some were departing passengers standing behind the railing of the deck and waving to friends and family on the dock. Smiling people stood next to crying people. Young and old, tall and short, well dressed and shabby. What a mixture of people stood on that deck!

I could hardly wait to get on this floating city and see what adventures awaited.

# Playtime on the High Seas

Picture this scenario. You are a five-year old child, born and raised in a tiny provincial German town in the 1930's, and you find yourself on an ocean liner—the world's largest playground. Think about it. An ocean liner has finite boundaries; so you can't really get lost. The dangerous areas on the ship have locked doors or big red "Do Not Enter" signs to keep out passengers.

So much to look at and learn about: the wide, richly carpeted staircases which led from one deck to another and then to the staterooms; the game rooms where adults played chess, cards, and other games; the inviting children's play room with its wind-up toys, games, large pillows, dolls and animals of all sizes and shapes; the salons with large windows overlooking the top deck where the grownups had cocktails, snacks, and talked to each other. Best of all was the beautiful dining room with its lovely crystal chandeliers. The tablecloths on the round tables were white linen damask. The water goblet at each place setting had a pastel color napkin arranged in it. The napkins were different colors at breakfast, lunch, and dinner. In the center of each table was a small cut glass bowl of fresh flowers. What an amazing variety of places for a child to explore!

When Mama, Papa, and I trudged up the gangway onto the *S.S. Deutschland,* I watched all the activities going on around us. Many people were getting on the ship. Some were being seen off by their friends and families. Even as a small child, I remember sensing the intense emotions felt by all of us as we left our homeland to start a new life in a new country far across the seas, speaking a new language and learning new ways to live.

On the ship's deck, I noticed smiling young men in dark blue uniforms and crisp white shirts scattered about. Each of them had a long sheet of paper in his hand. One of them strode up to us and said, "Welcome aboard the *Deutschland.* I'm Eric. Tell me your name, and I'll show you to your cabin."

"Joseph and Hanna Stern, and our daughter, Ruthie," replied Papa.

"Oh yes! Here you are on my list. Follow me." He tucked the paper into his breast pocket, took Mama's two suitcases with a swift friendly gesture, and led us towards the middle of the ship where a broad staircase appeared. Down one set of stairs and then another, down a long hall with numbered doors on each side and a multi-colored patterned carpet on the floor, around a corner, three more doors, and then Eric said, "Here we are. Cabin 396, your quarters for the next week. This cabin is in my area. I will be your steward. If you need anything, let me know; and I'll do my best to get it." He opened the door to the stateroom. I eagerly looked inside and saw a compact room where everything was neat and orderly. There were two regular size beds and a small one for me underneath the little round window that Eric called a porthole. Even a closet, two night tables, and a small bath. I was fascinated when I noticed that everything was attached to the walls or the floor. I soon found out why.

Lunch was served as a buffet in one of the salons. People were arriving, settling into their cabins. Lots of commotion. Not a time for elegant dining. I found plenty of good food to eat. All kinds of breads from dainty curved croissants to chunks of dark pumpernickle, cheeses, meats, and a variety of sausages, cottage cheese, pickled cucumbers and tomatoes, olives, cooked fruits, and fancy desserts—it made my mouth water just looking at them.

The ship had just started its voyage to Southampton, England. Even though the January skies were gray and blustery, and I could hear the noisy wind outside, we didn't feel any movement on board YET.

After lunch, Mama and Papa went back to the cabin and unpacked some clothes. Mama found room for them in the closet and in the drawers next to the closet. After all, none of us wanted to rummage through our stuffed suitcases for a week. "Mama," I pleaded, "Can I go for a walk on the top deck? I know how to get back to our cabin."

Mama looked like she was ready to say no, but Papa reassured her. "Ruthie will be fine, Hanna. Let her go."

Mama dressed me in my warm maroon hat and coat. When I looked sufficiently bundled up, she reluctantly turned me loose. I ran up the two flights of stairs and found myself on the main deck. Looking up and down, I only saw two people sitting outside on deck chairs. The rest of the chairs were folded up and leaning against the walls. As I approached them, I happily noticed they were teenagers. They smiled and called me over.

"We're Eva and Aaron Rosenthal on our way to study in England," explained the young blue eyed girl whose dark curls framed her lovely face. At the time I didn't know that many Jewish families who could not get out of Germany sent their children abroad to study and, hopefully, to survive.

"My name is Ruthie Stern, and we are going to Chicago in America."

Both the boy and girl laughed loudly. "We've been looking at this book on how to learn American English, and it has place names in it. There are funny places in America. Sit down and we'll tell you ones we just learned," said Aaron. He was not as fragile looking as his sister. He, too, had curly black hair; but his large head sat squarely on a sturdy body. "Our favorite so far is Mis-sis-sip-pi. We like Cin-cin-nat-i, too. And then there's Al-bu-quer-que."

I sat down and giggled at the funny words. "Why can't they name places like we Germans do—nice simple words like Berlin, Hamburg, Frankfurt? Americans must be odd people."

Eva commented, "When I first saw you walking towards us, I thought you must be a little Japanese girl with your short, straight, dark hair cut in bangs across your forehead." She told me that hairstyle was popular in the Orient. Even then I must have had an interest in other cultures because I thought it would be very exotic to be a Japanese girl and made a note to tell my parents what Eva said when I returned to Cabin 396.

Soon we were all getting cold. We walked into the game room, and they taught me to play a simple card game quite a lot like the game we call "Fish." We talked about where they lived in Frankfurt, a metropolitan city, and where I lived in Nieder-Ohmen, a rural village. The differences between our backgrounds and our ages melted away on that charmed afternoon of laughing, playing, and talking.

The wind had picked up. The waves were high, and the ship was rolling. When I opened the cabin door, I noticed my mother was lying on the bed, and her face was pale. Papa greeted me and explained, "Your mama seems to be a little seasick. She'll probably feel better after she eats."

That was not to be. Mama didn't get better. She got worse and worse. Soon she didn't even go upstairs to have meals. Papa would bring her food like bouillon and Zwieback toast. Sometimes she'd eat it, and sometimes, she wouldn't. I, on the other hand, was well and happy. The North Atlantic storms left me completely unaffected. For the first few days, I ate dinner with Papa at the table assigned to us. The wind howled, and icy hail pummeled the deck and made noise as it hit the portholes. I enjoyed it all. The decks rolled when you walked on them. Just another challenge for a five year old. By midweek, Papa was affected, too.

They both worried about what to do about me. Eric came to the rescue. He told the Captain about my plight; and that very evening, I ate at the Captain's table. What fun it was! The young officers and other guests questioned me and even listened to my responses. I told them about my Uncle Meier and Aunt Hedwig and two cousins. I told them how much I loved Rosie, the cow. I told them how the government had taken away my developmentally slow aunt and put her in a hospital and how I hoped she had made friends there. I felt ever so important and grownup, in fact, the most important I ever felt in my first five years of life. And I'll tell you something Mama never found out. The Captain and his friends would let me eat two or even three desserts if I wanted them. Mama NEVER let me do that.

I was sad when Aaron and Eva left the ship at Southampton. The ship took on more food, flowers, and passengers. We were at the dock for a long time. I watched for some children to play with, but couldn't find any. I did see a man and woman with a baby in their arms. I liked babies and thought I'd look for them later.

Being at Southampton was a welcome reprieve for my seasick mother. Both parents came to the lunch buffet, which I learned was the way we ate when we were in a port because the ship's crew was busy with many jobs. I took Mama and Papa on a tour of all the fascinating places I had found to explore on the ship.

But then the ship was on its way again and into the path of more winter storms. First Mama and then Papa spent time leaning over the deck railings and throwing up. I felt sorry for them, sort of; but I was having such a good time eating at the captain's table and being able to go where I wanted that I secretly wanted them to stay sick.

As the week passed, I seemed to get more and more energy. Exhilarated, I dashed here, bounded there, skipped down the long hallways. When the ship rolled in the waves, my feet would leave the deck's wooden floor, and it felt like flying. Steward Eric introduced me to his friends. Wherever I was on the ship, a steward would say something like "Ah, there goes Ruthie making her rounds!" and smile at me.

When I think about it now, I realize that I was relishing this incredible freedom from parental control, the first I had ever had.

On the evening before our arrival in New York, the Captain said, "I have something to remind you of the Atlantic voyage with us when you are living far from the ocean in Chicago." He reached over and gave me a wind-up duck that was about eight inches tall, dressed in an orange and blue outfit. I was so happy that my new friend gave me a present. That duck became one of my most prized possessions.

That night the seas turned calm, and we awoke to much excitement on board. You could hear the passengers' footsteps in the hallways as they hurried to the top deck. No one wanted to miss seeing the Statue of Liberty. The three of us joined the climbing throng of bodies. "Look! It's over there!" shouted Papa as he lifted me high. All I could see was a dark tall object far away in the water. As we watched, the Statue became the majestic figure of a woman in flowing robes holding aloft a flaming torch welcoming us to the United States as she had welcomed so many immigrants before us.

As we walked down the slanting gangway, I thought about the kind Captain and the friendly stewards. I felt pampered and petted, filled with delicious food, and the strong knowledge that there are lots of good people in the world. What a glorious adventure! I was ready to start life in America.

# The First Two Days in the USA

When my father, my mother, and I disembarked from the *Deutschland*, the ship that brought us to America on the stormy January ocean in 1939, I kept turning around to smile and wave at the stewards and the young officers standing on the deck in their blue uniforms and looking very smart as they said goodbye to the passengers. The ship's staff had been so kind to me. A part of me wanted to stay on the ship, race around the decks, eat desserts in the beautiful dining room, and feel like I was independent, even though I was only five years old.

But, no, we were on solid ground once more and being led to the immigration offices. My mother had all the papers clasped tightly in her hands. Our turn came. She handed everything to the tall, thin, middle-aged man in still another uniform. I wondered if most adults in the world wore uniforms. He carefully checked all the information and said "So! You're headed for Chicago, eh?" My mother heard "Chicago" and nodded even though she had no idea what he said. After we finished with him, we saw the doctors to make sure that we didn't have any serious illnesses. We didn't. And then we were outside where it seemed to me thousands of eager faces scanned each of us looking for their relatives. I don't know how my Uncle Albert found us, but he did.

"Welcome to America, Joseph, Hannah, and Ruthie!" Someone was speaking to us in German. We turned around, and there he was—a short, round, balding man wearing a striped suit. He had a mustache, which looked like a black line drawn on his upper lip. Uncle Albert was an accountant, who had been in New York for about ten years and knew his way around. He quickly hailed one of the many waiting taxicabs. Papa, Uncle Albert, and the driver stowed our luggage in the trunk. It took a bit of moving bags around before everything fit. The cab drove down busy streets. I watched the many pedestrians hurrying along. They were wearing thick coats, scarves, and gloves—all to protect them from the cold January winds.

As we turned a corner, Uncle Albert said, "Here we are at my American home. This building has 15 stories in it, and I live in an apartment on the fourth floor." The driver held the cab door open, and I got out and looked up. The brown brick building seemed immense—so many windows on each floor.

I thought, *There must be more people in this building than in all of Nieder-Ohmen.* When we crowded ourselves and our four suitcases into the small elevator, Uncle Albert said, "There's not going to be room for me this time. Ruthie, you'll be the operator. When the door is closed, press the "4" button." That made me feel important. Of course, I followed directions perfectly. When we exited the elevator, we saw a long hall with numbered doors on each side. The hall was painted deep gold, and the carpet with flowers in shades of maroon, green, and gold had seen lots of wear. There were no windows, and the whole effect was rather dark and gloomy.

Uncle Albert was a bachelor, and his apartment was just big enough for one—certainly not for three extra visitors. Fortunately, we were only going to be there for two days. The next days were a blur to me. I don't remember seeing anything of New York City at all. I do remember a series of visitors, other immigrants who knew my parents. The most memorable was Sigmund Stern, who was a waiter in a fancy restaurant. He came to visit us on his way home from work, and he wore an elegant tuxedo. *Gosh!* I thought, *That's the best uniform I've seen so far!* Sigmund was an outgoing man, who had been a friend of two of my mother's brothers. He was filled with stories about their teenage adventures. I heard about the time they took my grandfather's hay wagon, filled it with their friends, food and beer and had a party in the distant meadow. He talked about the girls he and my Uncle Leo liked. Of course, he insisted that his sweetheart was the most beautiful girl in town. I was charmed by him and warmed by the laughter welling up in my parents as they listened. Some of the strain left their faces, and they visibly changed their posture from stiff to relaxed as the visit continued.

The best part about seeing all those visitors was that many of them brought chocolate candy for me. I loved chocolates then and still do today. Even though I went to sleep with a stomachache both nights, it was a happy stomachache.

# A New York City Excursion

Papa sat on Uncle Albert's brown velour couch and read the German newspaper. In his heart and mind, he was still in Nieder-Ohmen, and he compulsively devoured everything he could find to tell him what was happening in Europe. *Why? Why?*, he wondered, *did the Germans follow Hitler so blindly? Didn't they remember all the Jews who fought valiantly for Germany in the First World War? My brother, Meier, and I both fought in that war. We were good citizens,* he thought. *We helped our neighbors. We paid our taxes. Why is this persecution happening? I don't understand.*

While Papa was in deep thought, Mama, the practical person in our family, talked to Uncle Albert. "We need food to take on the bus trip to Chicago," she said anxiously.

"That's easy. There's a grocery store on the corner. I'll take you there. Do you want to come along, Joseph and Ruthie?"

"No. I want to read the paper," Papa replied in a far away voice. I imagined he was seeing the gently rolling hills around our house in Germany and remembering how we would go for walks when the hay was just cut in the meadow and smell that wonderful aroma of freshly cut hay.

"I want to go!" I yelled. Sitting around the small apartment and listening to the grownups talk was boring, and I was ready to go anywhere. Sure, I knew it was cold and blustery, but I didn't care. I just wanted to be outside and run around.

"This grocery store has been here for many, many years," explained Uncle Albert as we saw the sign he translated as "Goldstein's Grocery". He held open the door, and we entered a long, narrow store. On one side there was a slanted counter with mirrors behind it. Piled neatly were shiny red apples, green apples, red and green apples, cauliflowers, green cabbages and purple cabbages, orange carrots with lacy green tops tied in bunches, large tan potatoes and little round pink potatoes, yellow and deep purple onions, and crisp white bulbs of garlic. Above the counter, there were shelves with many, many different grocery items, most of which I had never seen before. *Do people really eat so many things out of boxes?* I wondered? In Germany most of our food came from the garden, and I'd go with Papa to get vegetables for dinner in the summer. In the winter, we ate vegetables Mama had canned that were neatly lined up on a table in our cellar. There they were in clear jars; and I could see what was inside—tomatoes, peas, beans.

Then I noticed that on the other side of the store, there were shelves with cans that had pictures of peas, beans, yellow kernels that I later learned were called "corn". Below the shelves stood large wooden barrels, full of dill pickles, green tomatoes and other unrecognizable delicacies. The store was filled with the odor of smoked fish, garlic, and pungent spices.

Mama, with her usual focused attitude, murmured to herself, "Let's see, we will need food that won't spoil since we'll be on the bus for a day and a night. I will buy some cheeses, fruit, sausage and smoked fish."

"What about eggs? We'll hard boil them," suggested Uncle Albert.

"Good idea," agreed Mama.

"Oh, please, can you buy some pickles," I begged, as the pickle odor seduced me with longing. Mama made tasty pickles, and I wanted to try the ones here to see if they were as good.

Uncle Albert jumped in. "Sure we can! You can eat one now, and the rest can take the ride to Chicago with the three of you. They won't spoil."

"Oh, goody!" I exclaimed, as Uncle Albert went to find a clerk. The short, dark young man was wearing a soiled white apron that covered him from chest to knees. He had a large piece of brown paper in his left hand. With his right, he reached for the tongs attached by a wire to the side of the fat wooden pickle barrel and pulled out six juicy pickles. He smilingly gave me one, wrapped the others and gave them to Mama. I sank my teeth into the crisp green pickle and felt the juice trickle down my chin. *Oh my! This is the best pickle I've ever tasted. What should I do? Tell Mama or not?*

Before I could decide, Mama observed, "That American pickle must be something special. I can tell by looking at you." She chuckled, "Maybe I'll have to learn to make American pickles."

We walked to the delicatessen counter and saw sausages of many sizes, salami, slabs of corned beef and pastrami, chopped liver and chopped herring.

The counter man wore another soiled white apron. He was much older, perhaps Mr. Goldstein himself. "Good morning. What can I do for you?" He had a hearty voice with a strong Yiddish accent.

Uncle Albert explained, "My sister-in-law and niece are shopping for food to take on the bus to Chicago tomorrow, and they keep Kosher".

"Don't worry! I'll wrap the meat and the dairy products separately. All the food in this store meets the standards. Many observant Jews shop here."

I noticed that there was another counter that had many different kinds of cheese. They ranged in color from deep orange to soft white. Some of them had little holes, and one big chunk was filled with large holes. This counter had tubs of sour cream, cottage cheese, herring in sour cream, and salads that we didn't eat in Germany.

The grocer reached under the counter and got two large brown paper bags. In the first one he put the salami, corned beef and pickled tongue that he sliced on the large metal slicer behind the counter. I was fascinated as the thin slices piled up on the waxed paper he placed on the slicer tray. The slices were so thin and even. I had never seen a slicer before. Then he went to the dairy counter and carefully took the cheeses that my mother pointed out and sliced them on a different slicer. The cheese was put into a separate bag.

Uncle Albert and I picked out some apples. I liked the red and green ones that I had tasted at his house. He told me they were called "Macintosh apples." The insides were white and very juicy.

Loaded down with our purchases, we headed back to the apartment building. Mama and Uncle Albert carried the bags, and I skipped ahead in high spirits. I had a big smile on my face, and a chocolate colored woman pushing a fancy baby carriage smiled back at me. Maybe all would be well in this new country after all.

# The Bus Ride to Chicago

Thank goodness Uncle Albert paid for the taxi from his apartment to the Greyhound Bus station. We certainly could never have afforded it since we were only able to take 75 German marks out of the country. Even in 1939, that wasn't much money.

What a cold, blustery day it was! The sky was a lifeless gray, and a strong wind blew my pink knit scarf across my face as we left the taxi and entered the bus terminal. A steady stream of men, women, and children entered the building. They were bundled up against the January weather. When I looked at the grownup faces, I saw uncertainty and apprehension. We children were looking around, amazed at all the hubbub.

The station was crowded with people speaking many languages. My parents recognized German, Czech and Polish. There were languages they couldn't identify. Many of the others were immigrants like us going to places where their sponsoring families lived. At that time, the immigrants' relatives had to sign a guarantee that the newcomers would not be a burden to United States taxpayers. If we needed help, our extended family would have to provide it. The would-be passengers showed the agents scraps of paper with destinations scrawled on them. As we waited in line, we heard place names—"Omaha, Nebraska; Cleveland, Ohio; Savannah, Georgia." We had no idea where those places were, and they didn't either, but that's where their family was, and that's where they were going. Our family lived in Chicago; and that's where we were going.

My mother bought the tickets. She had practiced saying "Chicago" slowly and clearly. *Such a strange word,* she thought. With the tickets clutched in her hands, she led us towards the large opening through which I could see the colorless gray sky. My! So many shiny silver colored buses! Each stood expectantly next to a numbered platform and waited for its passengers. The Chicago bus left from Platform No.9. I was pleased since I thought of "9" as my lucky number. I stared at the huge silver beast with headlights that looked like eyes and a bumper that reminded me of a mouth. *This bus has a personality,* I thought. *It is dignified and reliable.* The side of the bus opened up, and the passengers put their luggage into its bowels. A trim gray uniformed man with thick brown hair and hazel eyes stood by the passenger door, took our tickets, and said, "Welcome to the Greyhound bus bound for Chicago. I'm, Mac, your driver."

When we heard "Chicago," my parents relaxed. At least we had arrived at the right bus. Now to find seats and put the bags of food underneath our feet so they would be easily accessible as we traveled. The seats were arranged in pairs. Mama and I sat on the left side of the bus, and Papa sat across the aisle. Mama gave me the window seat. I was delighted. I wanted to see what this enormous country looked like. I knew that we were going to the "Midwest", wherever that was, and that we were now on the "East Coast." I figured that if I kept looking out the window, everything would become clear to me.

Other passengers were getting on the bus. Most were bundled up against the January chill in dark heavy coats, Fedora hats for the men, woolen shawls for some of the immigrant women, leather gloves for the grownups, and home knit mittens for the children. Some of the mittens were in bright colors, and I liked the splashes of vividness enlivening the drab group. They stood in line waiting to get on—families with small children, worried looking gray-haired older people, men in dark blue denim work clothes, and a few couples who looked dressed up to me. These women wore coats of soft pastel wool with fur collars, and the men's topcoats fitted well. Their hats were the same color as their coats. They looked like they had thought about their appearance. I knew they must be Americans. The refugees, like us, carried their bags of food for the long ride. I didn't notice the Americans carrying any food.

The bus filled up in a hurry. No empty seats at all. The noise level was high and excited. Everyone was talking at once. Who could blame us? We were "strangers in a strange land" and we had no idea what awaited us. The chatter was a way to relieve our nervous tension.

The bus started with a mighty roar as Mac warmed it up on the cold winter morning. In a few moments it slowly made its way out of the station into the crowded streets of New York. People were everywhere. I enjoyed looking at people; so I was content to sit there with my palms glued to the window glass and my head propped up between them. After awhile the downtown crowds thinned out, and we were driving through a neighborhood with apartment buildings and small stores—butcher shops, groceries and laundries. I could see into the stores. Some were filled with customers. Others had just one or two people in them. Housewives carrying bulging shopping bags walked from shop to shop. Dirty snow was piled along the curbs. Next, I saw houses separated from each other by snowy yards and bare branched tall trees, their dark trunks contrasting starkly with the whiteness. "Oh look" I exclaimed to Mama, "an *Oma* (Grandma) is walking a cute beige colored dog with long floppy ears!" Some of the bushes close to the houses had a few straggly brown leaves still hanging on them. Then we were in open country covered by a blanket of fresh white snow that glistened in the occasional bursts of sunlight fighting their way through the gray clouds. Occasionally, I could see a prosperous white house next to a large red barn surrounded by lots of fields. That surprised me. In Germany, the houses were all in the villages; and the farmland was on the outskirts. Here the farmhouses were in the middle of the land. Didn't those people get lonely with no neighbors to talk to?

Gosh! The landscape was pretty—pristine white with gently rolling hills all around. I was so busy looking out,

I forgot to play with my doll, Heidi, who was sitting on my lap. I think she was looking out, too.

Soon there were woods every so often. As the hills became higher, I saw Christmas trees just like they had in Germany. We called them *tannenbaums*. Even though I was Jewish, I loved them because they were festive and beautiful when decorated with candles, brightly colored shiny balls, little carved and painted figures. These trees were growing and weren't decorated, but they were green and stood out in the gray woods. They looked so pretty accenting the snowy countryside. I secretly wished we could have one in our house. Mama would be angry if she knew. When Papa sang the "*Oh Tannenbaum*" song, she would firmly tell him to stop singing Christmas carols.

I don't know how long we had been riding the bus when Mac pulled into a parking lot at the side of the road. The sign said "Bill's Diner." "Bathroom and food stop," Mac called out, opened the bus door, and stood next to it to help the passengers off. Some immediately put on their coats and hats and trudged down the bus aisle. Mama, Papa and I looked out the window at the one story building that looked like a silver railroad car.

We slowly put our wraps on, and then we, too, got off the bus. As soon as the cold air hit my body, I wanted to go to the bathroom, and we went inside. Uh oh! There was a long line at the women's bathroom. I hopped on one foot and then the other. A young woman standing in line ahead of me laughed and motioned for Mama and me to go ahead. The round middle-aged woman wearing a gray shawl ahead of her did the same. In just a few minutes, I was in the bathroom, with my mother putting toilet paper on the seat to protect me from germs.

When we returned to the diner, Papa was seated on a stool with a cup of coffee lightened with a large amount of milk in front of him. He had draped his tan scarf knit by Mama on the stool to the right of him, and his brown fedora hat sat jauntily on the stool to the left. The plump, grinning waitress in a starched pink uniform was waiting on another of the bus passengers. In a few moments, she was in front of us asking, "What'll you have?" Mama shyly pointed to Papa's coffee. She nodded and said, "Okay, and I'll bring some cocoa for the little girl." When I heard "cocoa", I clapped my hands. That word is similar to the German. In Germany I drank the chocolate drink all winter long. It was especially delicious with Rosie's rich creamy milk. How I missed seeing her every evening and stroking her face as I told her what make believe games I had played, what I ate for lunch, and everything else that had happened while she was in the pasture at the edge of town.

The shiny red stool turned on its base, and I twirled around and around as I drank the cocoa. Frankly, it tasted watery; but it was so warm and sweet that it went down easily. Soon I noticed that the bus passengers were starting to get back on the bus. When we finished our drinks, we did the same.

I plopped into my seat next to the window, nestled Heidi into my lap, took off my coat and waited for Mac to start the engine. The light was getting softer. Perhaps there was some mist in the air. I noticed that the world outside was taking on a shimmering pink glow as the scattered sunlight reflected from house windows in the little towns caressed the stately trees, the bare bushes and the snow covered fields. *How peaceful it looks*, I thought. *Is that why all the immigrants want to come to America?*

Dusk comes early in January, and soon I could only see faint outlines of houses, barns, and an occasional car on the road. Mama had brought some blank white paper and a yellow pencil. I decided to teach Heidi her

"A, B, C's." I wrote the letters and then gave Heidi an example of a word for each letter. "A" is for "apfel." "B" is for "ball."

Mama rummaged in the food bag under her seat and brought out sliced kosher salami, rye bread and a crisp green pickle for me to eat for supper. I grabbed the pickle and ate it first. Oh! It was tasty. I took more time eating the sandwich. In a little while, she handed me some freshly cut and juicy apple slices on which I munched contentedly as the towns, fields and woods slipped silently by—now covered by a blanket of darkness. Uncle Albert had given us three *Life* magazines to look at on the journey. There were photos on every page—many of them of serious men talking to other serious men. I liked the pictures of attractive young people on the pages that were advertisements for products. They were lively and looked like they were having fun. After awhile, the people in the ads seemed to move on the page. The young people waved and talked directly to me. "*Wie gehts*, Ruthie?" Soon I became drowsy and slept in my seat with my head on my mother's shoulder.

The sky was medium blue, but the sun was nowhere to be seen when I awoke the next morning. Mama and Papa were both asleep, slumped in their seats. Mama's mouth was open, and she looked funny. I pulled the sleeve of her dress, and she woke up. "Good morning, Mama. Will we be in Chicago soon?"

"Not until this afternoon", she answered. "America is a big country. If we were in Germany, we'd be in Poland or France or Holland by now, but here we are still in America. This country goes from the Atlantic to the Pacific Ocean. Think of that!"

I looked out the window and saw flat land with houses closer together than yesterday. There were large buildings with tall smoke stacks spewing out black smoke that spiraled up into the sky. On the land near the large buildings, there were big trucks. Often the large buildings were near railroad tracks, and boxcars stood waiting to be filled with goods made inside the buildings. Papa said the buildings were factories, perhaps steel mills. I didn't know what steel mills were; so he told me that steel was used to make buses, ships, and ovens. Now that I knew how useful steel mills were, I looked at them with more interest. Sometimes I thought I saw flames coming from inside the building. Papa said fire is used to make steel. I decided that I certainly didn't want to be a worker who had to tend the hot flames. America is a bustling country, we decided. So many factories! So many trucks! So many workers going to work, each with a black metal container that Mama said held their lunch.

The passengers were waking up, and the silent bus became filled with the hum of morning small talk. "Breakfast stop coming right up, folks," announced an unfamiliar voice with a slight foreign accent. "That doesn't sound like Mac! Where's Mac?" I asked nervously. I liked Mac and somehow felt safe with him driving the huge bus.

Mama gently explained "Mac drove the bus until the last stop of the evening. Then he got off and went to be with his family. Now he has had a good night's sleep, and he's probably playing with his children. You wouldn't want him to drive all night. He might have become so tired that he would have had an accident."

I put my chin on the window ledge and peered out the window. Yes, there was another silver diner by the side of the road. The sign on this one read "Jimmy and Betty's Diner". All the passengers knew the routine by now—put on your coats and hats, get off the bus and get in the bathroom line first. Then get food and drinks.

Passengers ordered scrambled eggs. Mama and Papa decided to splurge and get some. They pointed to the eggs when the waitress came to take their order. I helped

Mama eat hers. We all had healthy appetites and cleaned every morsel of food from the plates.

"Chicago bus leaving!" called the new driver with firm dignity. Everyone returned to the bus. Some of the older folks ambled slowly. The younger people walked briskly. We children skipped and ran, racing to see who would get there first. Like Mac, this driver stood by the side of the bus as we ran up to the bus laughing—our faces red from the cold air. His smile was tentative—like he knew he was supposed to smile, but deep in his heart, he didn't feel like it. "I am Yanek," he told us and tipped his cap to us and to my parents who were following close behind the small group of bouncy children. I looked him over. He was short for a man and round. His head was round. His glasses were round. His belly was round and lopped over his belt—not a lot, just a little. He wore the same gray uniform that Mac wore, but he looked different in it. Yanek wasn't handsome like Mac, but he had soft, sad brown eyes and looked like a kind, gentle man. He spoke some Yiddish and some Polish. The Yiddish was enough like German for me to understand a little of what he said to us. "This afternoon you will start your new life in Chicago," he said to my parents in Yiddish. My papa smiled to be acknowledged by Yanek.

"Yes, a new life. What will it be like? How can a small town cattle dealer find a job in a large industrial city?" he hesitatingly replied in German.

"Don't worry. You'll find something to do. Look at me. In Poland I was a violinist in an orchestra. Here I am driving a bus. But I still play music with my friends from the old country and find ways to be content. You will, too. I guarantee it!" He gave my father a friendly smile and patted him on the shoulder.

Now I liked Yanek. Anyone who makes Papa feel better is my friend. I took his hand when he helped me on the bus and smiled at him. He smiled back and told me "You will go to school in Chicago, and soon you'll be speaking English like a native."

I remembered my papa telling me that the natives were Indians. "Did the Indians speak English?" I asked. His eyes sparkled, as he replied, "No, they didn't. The immigrants from England, immigrants just like you, brought English with them. America is a land where immigrants have landed since the 1600's and made a new life for themselves. Your mama and your papa and you will do the same thing."

I nodded as I walked down the bus aisle and found my seat next to the window. It was easy to find our seats. I just looked for the brown paper bags sticking out underneath. Out of curiosity, I opened the two bags. The food supply was smaller now, but there were hard boiled eggs, apples, cheese, dark bread in one, now crinkled, bag and two pickles, salami and rolls in another. Knowing there was food to nibble on made me feel secure somehow even though I wasn't the least bit hungry.

I settled into my seat and took Heidi out of the cloth bag that Mama had made for her. She and I nestled in. Sometimes when the bus stopped, passengers would leave the bus, and we would wish them well. The English words that people were using sounded like "Bi! Goud luk" We said, *"Auf wiedersehn!* (Till we meet again!)"

We were in "Ohio." I thought, *that rhymes with Chicago. Must be another Indian word.* I amused myself by saying "Ohio Chicago." Then we arrived in Toledo, where five passengers, including a little girl named Katya, who was three years old, got off. We ran around when the bus stopped. I was sorry to see her go, but now I had another word for my rhyme—"Ohio, Toledo, Chicago". I said it to myself over and over. It kept me amused as I looked out the window and saw gray snow piled at the edges of street curbs, large buildings with fences around them and big trucks and railroad yards with lots of tracks filled with quietly standing freight cars—both empty and filled with black rocks or sand. Sometimes we passed lakes, rivers and ponds. That was fun because I watched for ducks, geese, and boats. I was ready to get to Chicago. The scenery was getting to be more and more of the same. Factories with smoke spewing out of smoke stacks, large buildings two and three stories high, piles of dead automobiles laying in heaps half covered with melting snow. I felt sorry for them. The cars looked like they had been abandoned by families who loved them once-upon-a-time.

I asked Papa about the sad cars. He explained, "Ruthie, the cars will be melted down and the steel used to make new cars." Somehow, that explanation made me feel better.

"Indiana!" Yanek called out that the bus was in Indiana. I liked seeing the farms we drove by. Sometimes Mama, Papa, or I would catch sight of a black and white cow, a few sheep in their wooly winter coats, or a horse. Whoever saw any animals would tell the others. As we got closer and closer to Chicago, there were fewer farms and more factories. Gary, Indiana, was full of big factories.

Soon we would arrive in Chicago. The excitement among all of us permeated the bus like the smell of a strong perfume. Will Cousin Irving actually be there to meet us? What if he isn't? Mama had the addresses of Cousin Goldie, Cousin Lily, and Aunt Dina. So, she knew we could make our way to one of the houses if no one showed up at the station. Still, we had so little money. That would be a big problem.

The highway was crowded with traffic, and the short January day had turned to twilight when Yanek announced, "We have crossed the city limits into Chicago, Illinois." Getting through the city to the downtown bus station took forever. I looked at the houses built close together. Some were built of bricks and some of wood. Many had front porches, and I could see lights on inside. Figures could be seen moving behind sheer curtains. Soon we saw apartment buildings like Uncle Albert's. Some areas had lots of brightly lit stores—all kinds—groceries, butcher shops, big stores with the word, "Sears" on the front, stores that sold clothes with statues of women in the windows. Mama had explained to me in Germany that women looked at the clothes on the statues, and if they liked them, they'd go into the shop and buy them. I was happy to see the statues because I knew what they were for.

Yanek shouted, "This is the Loop, the center of Chicago". The murmur on the bus increased. The immigrants realized we would get off the bus soon. There was no turning back. Mama looked around the seats to make sure nothing of ours was forgotten. The food bags were empty. High time to get to Chicago.

Brrrrr! It seemed colder here than in New York. The wind caused our eyes to tear as we retrieved our four bags from the insides of the bus after Yanek opened the door. We walked rapidly inside the station. What a contrast to the dark platform to walk into the large bright room filled with relatives waiting for their European families. We immigrants were alert and watchful. The families meeting the immigrants were alert and watchful. No one wanted to miss his or her relatives

We stood for a few moments inside the door taking in the scene. Slowly we started walking. A man appeared. He was holding a photo in his hand. "Joseph, Hanna, Ruthie!" You look just like your picture. We didn't know what he said, but he held out his hand to shake my father's and my mother's. I was given a friendly pat on the head. Thank goodness! Cousin Irving had come for us. We had crossed our first hurdle.

# Welcome to
# Your New Home

"We're here! We're here!" I felt like jumping up and down and shouting. I was happy to be on solid ground once more. I ran little circles around Mama and Papa as Cousin Irving picked up Mama's two suitcases, and Papa carried the other two. Cousin Irving led us out of the bus station into a large parking lot. The frigid wind went through our clothes and bellowed "Wake up!" to our tired bodies. When Cousin Irving opened the back door of his car, Mama and I climbed in rapidly while the suitcases were maneuvered into the trunk. Then, the men scrambled into the front seat, and we heard the unfamiliar sound of the car engine starting as we slowly drove out of the parking lot. Snuggled up next to Mama with no wind blowing in my face, I felt relaxed and comfortable.

Snowflakes started drifting out of the sky as Cousin Irving drove us along the Outer Drive to see the beautiful skyscrapers that line Michigan Avenue. Lights twinkled in building windows, and colorful neon signs shown brightly as we peered out of the car amazed by the nighttime beauty of the city. A breathtaking first view of Chicago!

We then headed for his mother's house. *Tante* Dina Gardner was my mother's youngest aunt. She had come to the United States with her sister, *Tante* Regina, before World War I. My mother knew her only when she was a small child. Dina was now a widow with two sons still living at home, Irving and Sol, and two married daughters, Goldie and Lily.

In 1939, people in the United States were struggling to recover from the Great Depression. Most people were poor. Irving was selling goods on credit from his car, and Sol was studying to be an accountant. In the apartment that Dina and the boys shared, there was no room for three extra guests. Cousin Goldie had found us a furnished room in which to live until we found something better.

That evening the whole family was at *Tante* Dina's small apartment awaiting our arrival. When we pulled up in front of a yellow brick three-story apartment building on the West Side, Mama took one of our suitcases upstairs with her. I knew it was filled with gifts for everyone, but Irving wondered why she insisted on bringing it up.

When the door swung open, I saw a sea of smiling, welcoming faces—old and young—and heard a mixture of German and Yiddish spoken. All the grownups hugged or patted me. The three children—two boys a few years older than I, and one girl perhaps a year younger, looked at me with friendly curiosity.

The women took our coats, hats, scarves, and gloves and took us to the dining room where a table was laden with cold cuts—corned beef, tongue, pastrami, and all the trimmings—potato salad, coleslaw, and rye bread. Plates were pressed into our hands, and we were encouraged to eat. No one had to persuade me! I was hungry, and I was happy to gobble down the sandwich Mama made for me. *This food is delicious,* I thought. Corned beef was a new taste delight for me—one that I enjoy to this day.

The adults talked about our sea voyage, Hitler, and the plight of the Jews in Europe, while the little girl, Helene, showed me her dolls and a tiny tea set. We smiled, nodded and played together even though I spoke no English and she spoke no German.

My mother had brought two silver fox furs for her cousins. The furs still had heads on them with little black beady eyes. I thought they were awful, but Goldie and Lily seemed delighted to have them and declared they would wear the fox stoles over their winter coats. Mama presented lovely embroidered tablecloths with matching napkins to *Tante* Dina and *Tante* Regina.

When we were satiated with food and companionship, Irving drove us to our temporary sleeping place—the furnished room in a nearby flat. The room contained a double bed and a small bed for me and was barely large enough for our luggage and us. But we were so tired by then, nothing mattered except having a place to lie down and sleep. In the middle of the night, I awoke feeling itchy. When I sat up, I noticed that my parents were awake, too. Sleepily, we turned on the light and saw dozens of little black bugs crawling on the white sheets. I was horrified! Never had I experienced what I soon learned were bedbugs. My parents now had a mission—to find an apartment and get out of that disgusting room. Within a week we had a tiny first floor apartment in the back of a building. The entrance was facing the alley instead of the street. Therefore, the rent was inexpensive.

My father had spent all week "pounding the pavement" to find a job—any job that would pay enough money so that we could buy food to eat and find another place to live. He walked into every store in the immigrant neighborhood in which we now lived and asked the proprietor if he had any work. The job he found was pulling the feathers off dead chickens in a kosher butcher shop. Not a job he wanted to keep for long, but it was good enough for now. Cousin Goldie knew a doctor's wife who wanted a house cleaner, and my mother gratefully accepted that job. Now the problem was—what were they going to with me after school?

Cousin Goldie to the rescue! She knew about the Douglas Park Day and Night Nursery where children could go for childcare after school. It was walking distance from Pope School. Within two weeks I was a first grade student who walked to the nursery after school. How fast things were happening!

My teacher was young and dedicated. I was the only non-English speaking child in her class. She was willing to work with me by saying the English names of objects in the classroom and writing them down for me. I learned to read and speak English rapidly, mainly because of the patient help of Miss Henneberry. As I began to speak

English, I became the spokesperson for my parents. When the faucet leaked, I called the landlord. When my parents wanted to start a bank account, I spoke to the teller. There wasn't much time for childhood play and frivolity in the life of little Ruthie.

My mother had read stories about the famous Chicago gangster, Al Capone, in the German newspapers. She knew he drove around in a big black roadster. She was sure Al Capone and other mobsters randomly drove about the city shooting people and were a danger to us. When we walked down the street and she noticed a large black car coming towards us, Mama would quickly pull me into the nearest doorway until the car had passed by. It took about a year of living in the Windy City before she stopped pulling me into doorways when big black cars drove by.

My immune system wasn't used to American germs. I developed a high fever and a rash that wouldn't go away. My worried mother called Goldie, who asked her doctor to come to our apartment to see me. Yes! In those days, doctors made house calls. He diagnosed me with a case of scarlet fever. This was serious. He nailed a quarantine notice to our front door and said I couldn't go out, and no guest could visit until I was not contagious. My mother was in a state of panic. What would happen to her job if she couldn't go to work? It was decided that Mama would make me breakfast and a sandwich for lunch. Then she would go to work. The first day home alone was very long even though Mama had gone to the library and brought home a big pile of books. When I heard Mama's key turn in the lock, I was so glad to see her. She had a package of chocolate cookies in her purse as a special gift.

That evening Papa brought home our very first radio to keep me company during the day. What a great present! He put it right next to my bed, and the following day I turned the dial from station to station until I found programs I liked. Chicago had a large immigrant population. I found German programs, along with Italian, Polish and Hungarian ones. Even when I couldn't understand the announcers' words, I enjoyed the music they played. The lively Polish polkas and the lyrical Italian melodies sung by tenors were my favorites. I was in complete control of it during the day, and it made the time go ever so much faster until I heard that welcome key turn in the lock. The radio became my constant companion and source of entertainment and information.

I wonder if those early radio experiences are the reason why I feel lonely if I don't have a radio playing during the day. The radio is as important to me now as it was when I was six and sick with scarlet fever.

# My Hero

What does a hero look like? Superman? Tarzan? King David?

My hero was a skinny fifteen-year-old kid named Alfred. His nose was too big for his long, narrow face. His curly hair was a mousy brown, and he wore thick glasses.

Alfred and I met at the Douglas Park Day and Night Nursery. I was a "day." That meant my parents picked me up after work. He was a "night." That meant he lived there all the time. Alfred was a "knight" in a more important way. He protected me from the hurtful cruelty of other children.

I started going to the Nursery soon after we arrived in Chicago in January, 1939, and my parents found jobs. I spoke only German—with a few English words thrown in here and there—"yes, no, hello, thank-you, okay, goodbye." The children at the nursery had heard their parents talking about the terrible things the German

Nazis were doing in Europe. I came from Germany; so I must be a Nazi.

As I walked to the nursery, I met other children going there, too. "Here comes the Nazi!" "Why don't you go back to the Fatherland?" "Dirty Nazi!" "We don't want you around here!" The taunts were shouted out. I ran to the door, rushed into the building, and found a corner in the playroom where I could look out the window. Even though I didn't make a sound, the tears streamed from my eyes.

Alfred, doing his homework at a desk facing the window, was the only one who noticed. He came over, put his hand on my shoulder, and quietly asked, "What's wrong, little girl?"

I cried even harder as I felt his gentle touch and heard his sympathetic voice. He heard me say "Nazi" and "Jude" between sobs. How ironic it was to have the Nazis drive us out of Germany, to come to America and be called a Nazi!

Alfred was puzzled and found an employee who spoke Yiddish, a language that has similarities to German. She translated my sobbing words for him. It took him just a few minutes to figure out the whole picture. I was being tormented by the older children.

I now had a protector. He kept me in his sight in the afternoons. Whenever he saw an older child approach me, he'd walk over and say to them, "If you insult Ruthie by calling her a Nazi, I'll deal with you. She left Germany *because* of the Nazis, you idiot!" It didn't take long for the word to get out. Alfred was watching over me. Since he was bigger and older than most of the other children, his word had clout.

For the rest of my stay at the Douglas Park Day and Night Nursery, my biggest complaint was having to eat creamed corn for dinner. Yuck! The children treated me with curiosity, and some even learned to like me.

There is a post-script to this story. Two years later, there was a knock on our apartment door. When my mother opened it, a thin young soldier stood in the hallway. "Hello, Mrs. Stern. I'm Alfred from Douglas Park. I want to tell Ruthie that I'm going to help rid the world of Nazis; so she never has to worry about being called a Nazi again." By then, I was standing next to my mother. He lifted me off my feet with his big hug and said, "When I fight the Nazis, I'll think of you.

I never saw him again.

# Blonde is Beautiful

The year was 1939. The United States was just starting to come out of the big depression. Jobs were scarce. What kind of work could Hanna and Joseph find? They had come from Nieder-Ohmen, Germany. He had been a cattle dealer. Back home, she had cooked the meals, cleaned the house, washed the clothes, planted the garden. None of these skills were sought after in Chicago. But wait—even in Chicago, people wanted clean houses.

And so my mother's first job was that of a cleaning lady. I remember one of her early customers was *Frau Doktor* Danielius. She was a doctor's wife, and my mother, being very impressed with people in authority, never called her *Frau* Danielius, but always *Frau Doktor* Danielius. I will call her *Frau* Danielius since I have been raised in the U.S. and have lost the extreme German respect for authority figures, thank goodness! Frau Danielius, quite unbeknownst to her, helped me learn about American culture. What she did was give my mother her outdated *Life* magazines. Every evening I poured over them. Being only five years old, I didn't read any of the articles, but I loved the ads.

I remember turning the pages of *Life* magazine and seeing photos of blonde, blue-eyed smiling young women. They were frequently surrounded by admiring young men.

I wanted to be like them.

This envy of blonde, blue-eyed girls—where in the world did it come from? My conjecture had always been that it was because I felt like an outsider in Chicago—this little girl with short, straight, dark hair and bangs which rested above her sad brown eyes. When I looked at those magazines, I assumed that blonde, blue-eyed girls were the ones approved of by society. After all, they looked so happy and confident in the photos.

That was too simplistic an answer. My cousin Karola told me a story about my childhood that tells me that the envy started much earlier. She said that when I was about three years old, she remembers when my cousin Sonia, who had blonde curly hair and blue eyes, came to Nieder-Ohmen. I looked at her with longing, walked up to her, stroked her hair and her face and said, "You are such a pretty girl."

My cousin remembers saying to me, "You, too, are a pretty girl." I just ignored her.

I wonder if I absorbed the Hitler propaganda of the superiority of the Aryan race. The Germans glorified that fair skinned, blonde, blue-eyed look as the ideal. Do cultural mores creep into the life of a young child at such an early age? Who can say?

I only know that feeling has been with me for as long as I can remember.

Then, while studying *Life* magazines in the United States, I learned "Blondes have more fun!" Doomed to be second-class by my Semitic looks, I decided to be smart instead. That early decision has shaped my life. Thank you, Frau Danielius.

# Settling In

Life was getting better for the Stern family in Chicago. Mama now had a job filling orders at the large catalogue company, Sears Roebuck. Their sprawling corporate headquarters were located within walking distance of our home. Sears sold merchandise from its catalogue all over the continent. They needed many order fillers, and my mother was hard working and accurate. Lucky for me, Sears gave an employee discount, and at the end of a season published a "Sale" catalog. Sometimes, when I needed a new dress, Mama and I would pick out an inexpensive, practical one that was on sale. I was thrilled to have an occasional dress that wasn't cut down from one of Mama's.

My mother was a naturally frugal, maybe even penurious, person and ran our household carefully. Every Wednesday evening, she scoured the grocery ads for the best bargains. On Thursday evenings after dinner she and I followed our weekly ritual by walking to the two neighborhood supermarkets pulling our collapsible-wheeled shopping cart. Each store was about a mile away, but not in the same direction. We stocked up on the groceries that were on sale that week. Candy, cookies, and other frivolous packaged items were out of the question.

I must give my mother credit. With her frugal management, she was able to save enough money to provide for my parents in their old age. My mother was determined they would make it on their own and not need help from the "government." They never did. On the other hand, they never bought things that might have brought them pleasure, such as music recordings or books. I don't ever remember them going out to dinner or to the movies. Those activities were too expensive in my mother's view of life. She thought WORK was the best way a person could spend their time. After I married and moved to Madison, Wisconsin, in our weekly telephone calls, she would sign off by saying, "Vell, go do your vork." With that message given by mother throughout my childhood, for years I felt guilty if I was having too much fun or spending money for "frivolous" things. I'm happy to tell you I eventually learned that having fun and spending money was acceptable, as long as I did it in moderation.

Papa looked at the Job Want Ads in the newspaper every Sunday. He and I read them together in case he didn't understand all the words. Besides, it was something for us to share doing. He noticed there were jobs in the Chicago Stockyards and applied for several before he landed one as a beef boner in a packing plant on the South Side. He now had to take public transit instead of walking to work, but he learned a new trade—that of cutting up large sides of beef into roasts and chops to be sold in butcher shops and grocery stores.

Best of all, we now had a "front" apartment. That meant it overlooked the street instead of the back alley. The flat was on the third floor of a fifteen-story unit, rather seedy brown brick apartment building located at 3216 Sixteenth Street on the corner of Sawyer Avenue in the middle of Chicago's West Side. The apartment came with a gas stove and an oak icebox. The iceman would come several times a week carrying a large square of ice on his shoulder and holding it firm with a pair of pincers. I remember him well. He was a short, muscular man who wore scuffed brown leather trousers and a leather vest. He placed a leather pad on his ice carrying shoulder to keep it dry. When he came to our house, he would cry out, "How is the beautiful princess feeling today?"

I would smile shyly and mumble, "Very well, thank you," as I had been taught in school. I was a good student, but I was timid and had little confidence in myself. Luckily, several girls my age lived on Sawyer Avenue and became my friends. We walked to Howland School together and sometimes played with each other in the afternoons. I was the only one whose mother worked away from home, and I spent many an afternoon at Barbara or Fern's house. Paper dolls were our chief form of amusement. They were modeled after famous movie stars, characters from novels, or foreign royalty. My favorite paper dolls were the ones of movie stars, and my VERY favorite was Hedy Lamarr. (I didn't know then that she and I had a lot in common. She was an Austrian Jewess who left Europe in 1938.) One day when we were having an argument, Barbara tore the head off Hedy. I was furious with her for weeks!

Barbara's family rented a vacation cottage in South Haven, Michigan for a week every summer. Since Barbara was the only girl in her family with two brothers, she asked me if I'd like to join their family on the trip and be her playmate. Would I? I'll say! Since we arrived in the United States, I had never been as far as the outskirts of Chicago, let alone to a different state. My parents gave their consent after my mother gave me enough advice for a year's journey instead of a weeklong outing! The cottage was simple, and we slept on the sun porch. Barbara's mother cooked "kid friendly" meals for us—macaroni and cheese, hot dogs, hamburgers and fried chicken. I didn't get that kind of food at home, and it was a treat. We were able to walk to the beach and play on the shore all day, digging in the sand, running in the waves and reading books as we relaxed on blankets. My very first American vacation was a big success, and I liked Barbara again—even if she had torn Hedy's paper head off.

Our lives had settled into a comfortable routine. School and work took up the weekdays. On Friday afternoon we got ready for *Shabbos* (the Sabbath). My mother worked until three o'clock on Friday. I helped her set the table and tear lettuce for the salad, while she prepared the chicken soup, roast chicken, cooked vegetables, and potatoes. We bought challah and cake for the dinner, and sweet rolls for *Shabbos* breakfast at the Jewish bakery on Kedzie Avenue since there wasn't time to bake after work. At sunset, my mother recited the *Shabbos* blessings over the candles, the wine and the challah before dinner was served.

On Saturday mornings Mama read the Sabbath morning prayers in her prayer book. When I was nine years old, she became concerned that I didn't know Hebrew and couldn't read the prayers. Now Mama read the prayer book in Hebrew fluently, but she had no idea what the words meant. She wanted me to learn to read, too. I was neutral to the idea, but being an obedient child, I voiced no objection to attending Hebrew school. We did not belong to a synagogue because Mama didn't want to pay the yearly membership fees since Papa was not interested in going to the synagogue to pray every week, and she liked praying at home. That meant she needed to find another way for me to learn Hebrew.

The solution was a little *cheder* (Hebrew School) in a storefront on Kedzie Avenue.

The only teacher was Mr. Katz. He was an elderly man with thinning gray hair, a lined face to match, and a protruding belly. His six or seven students were seated on wooden benches attached to tables that looked like miniature picnic tables. We were all there to learn our *Alef Bet* (Hebrew ABC's). Mr. Katz passed out first Hebrew books and lectured about the alphabet and vowels. Then we worked on our own until he came to help each of us individually. When he sat down next to me, he put his arm around me and breathed in my ear while having me read the simple Hebrew words. I felt really uncomfortable when he was close to me. What to do? *My mother wants me to learn Hebrew, but I hate the way I feel when Mr. Katz touches me,* I thought. *Mama will be angry if I quit. Well, I'll go back one more time.* The second week, Mr. Katz acted the same way. After class, I ran home, burst into the house and shouted, "I am NEVER going back to that Hebrew class again. Mr. Katz puts his arm around me and breathes in my ear. I don't like him! He makes me feel creepy!" My mother looked at me for a long time without saying a word. Finally, she said quietly, "All right, you don't have to go back."

What a revelation!! For the first time in my life, I realized that Mama would listen to me—that I had some ability to get her to see my side of things. I felt a sense of power that I used for the rest of my childhood—the power to tell an adult what was happening to me and perhaps get them to see it my way.

# My Fairy Godmother

Shhhhhh. I'll tell you a secret. I had a fairy godmother. She didn't look like Cinderella's fairy godmother. You know—long blonde hair, big blue eyes, a beautiful chiffon gown the same color blue as her eyes, and carrying a wand that had a sparkly star at the end—the Disney version. The important thing about fairy godmothers is they introduce you to a new magical world, one you never even knew existed.

My fairy godmother did that. She was a teacher named Mildred Anderson, who taught fifth grade at Howland Elementary School in Chicago. Mrs. Anderson was a woman of medium height in her mid—forties. She had permed short brown hair, and a warm smile that made her green eyes sparkle behind her tortoise shell glasses. She wore sensible black oxford shoes and prim skirts and blouses—a teacher of the 1940's. Mrs. Anderson was the first grownup in Chicago who thought I was special. For some unknown reason, she decided to take me under her wing. Perhaps Mrs. Anderson was ahead of her time. She decided to start her own "Head Start" program one student at a time. Although I was smart and did well in school, she may have noticed that other children talked about going on vacations, going to the zoo, going to museums. I never talked about those activities because I never did them!

When my parents arrived from Germany with their meager possessions and no money, their goals were to get jobs, find an apartment to rent, and build some security in their adopted home. Going places with me was far down on the "to do" list. By the time my father had worked in the stockyards and my mother had cleaned peoples' houses all week, their weekends were for relaxing and renewing their strength.

Mrs. Anderson called me into her office one recess. "Have you ever been to the arboretum, or the Museum of Science and Industry, or the Field Museum?"

"No, my parents don't do things like that. They don't speak English, and don't have a car," I explained. "They have never even heard of the museums".

"I would like to take you to some of those places on Saturday mornings. Chicago is an exciting city, and you're missing out on the excitement. Would you like to do that?"

I must have been speechless. I remember bobbing my head up and down. Spending alone time with my beloved teacher on Saturdays. How could I be so lucky?

"Good! I'll write a note to your mother. Now, there's one important rule you must obey. You may not tell the other children about our Saturday outings. If you do, they will think you're teacher's pet and tease you."

That afternoon I rushed home after school. My mother arrived from work two hours after I did. I heard her footsteps on the stairs and rushed out to the hallway to meet her. "Mama, Mama! Mrs. Anderson wants to take me to museums on Saturday mornings."

My mother was surprised and puzzled. Immediately, her face showed suspicion and uncertainty. "Why does she want to do this? What does she want with you?"

"She wants me to see Chicago. She knows we don't have a car; and we don't go to museums and other places that the American children go."

"But Ruth, Saturday is the Sabbath. We don't ride on the Sabbath. It is a day of rest."

I broke down into heartbroken sobs. "I have a chance to spend time with the best teacher in the whole world, and you would deny it to me. You're the cruelest mother who ever lived."

My mother was taken aback. She had rarely seen such an intense emotional outburst from me. She quietly said, "I'll talk to your father about this. We don't have to decide right now."

I could hardly wait for my father to come home. He entered the apartment in his soiled blue work pants and plaid shirt carrying his black metal lunch box. He headed for the bathroom to wash up. But, no. Before he could get to the bathroom door, I accosted him. "Daddy, something wonderful happened to me today. Mrs. Anderson said she wants to take me to see Chicago on Saturday mornings. Please, please! Say I can go."

My mother marched into the hallway and said, "Ruth, leave your father alone. We will talk about this during dinner."

I had trouble sitting still. Finally, my mother put the meat loaf, diced potatoes, and green beans on the table and sat down. Then my father sat down between us. "Now, what is going on?" he asked with a twinkle in his eye as he noticed how eager I was to talk to him.

"Well, I want to go with Mrs. Anderson to see the places in Chicago that I never get to see. She says that Chicago is an exciting city and that I'm missing out on the excitement. She thinks it will be good for my education."

My mother looked displeased and reminded my father, "Joseph, it's the Sabbath. It is against our religion. How can we do this?"

My father looked at my eager pleading face and replied. "Hanna, this is a big honor for our daughter. Let the child go."

I jumped up from the table and grabbed my father around the neck and hugged him. "Oh, thank you, thank you, Papa."

The first outing we took was to the Garfield Park Conservatory. There I saw cotton growing. It looked so much like the little cotton balls that we bought at the store. I was utterly amazed. The Saturday morning we traveled to Brookfield Zoo, I could hardly wait to see live elephants, lions, and tigers. And see them we did. The day was chilly and cool, and the zoo was un-crowded. We were right next to the cages. The giraffes were the biggest surprise. And I mean big. What huge, graceful creatures they were!

My fifth grade year was filled with thrilling anticipation of Saturday mornings with Mrs. Anderson. When I think back on that time, I realize what a turning point it was for me. Being with my beloved teacher and learning about the exciting, wonderful city of Chicago were much more important to me than obeying the Sabbath rules. The way I looked at it—my Saturday morning adventures did not interfere with my being Jewish. They enriched my life. How could God disapprove? God would want me to be happy, wouldn't he? And, besides, God must have created my fairy godmother just so she could introduce me to this new magical world—one that I never even knew existed.

# Back to the "Old Country"

Ruth and Grandchildren Katie and Rob
Shenon,
Saying Kaddish in Nieder-Ohmen (2008)

I made my first trip back to Nieder-Ohmen in
1979 accompanied by my husband, Burt, and my two

daughters, Amy, age 18, and Felicia, age 14. We were warmly welcomed by our former neighbors. None of them had been Nazis in the thirties, and they had helped us as much as they could even though it was dangerous to "fraternize with the Jews." As returnees to the "old country" will do, we brought gifts for them, including a book I had recently co-authored, *Helping Children to Like Themselves.*

In 2008—twenty-nine years later—my partner, Sam, my grandchildren, Katie, age 16, and Rob, age 14, and I made another trip to Nieder-Ohmen. Before our journey, I had contacted Heinrich Reighel, the volunteer town historian.

So, the community knew we were to visit. This time we were welcomed at a reception in the town hall by the mayor, the town historian, the director of social services, and residents who knew me as a child. We were interviewed and photographed, and our homecoming was reported in the regional newspaper. There was heartfelt conversation among us all, with remorse and guilt freely expressed by those who knew why my family had left so abruptly.

Heinrich and his wife, Kathe, showed us the photographs of Nieder-Ohmen boys who were drafted into the army and killed in World War II. My goodness!

There were so many of them for such a small town. And many looked about the age of my grandson—fourteen. I thought of the suffering of their parents and grandparents and cried. Kathe cried with me.

During the reception, we were told that *Helping Children to Like Themselves* had been translated into German and was being used to work with children to build self-esteem. Finding out about that was a big boost to my own self-esteem!

Let me tell you a little more about Nieder-Ohmen. It is located 90 kilometers northeast of Frankfurt-on-the-Main. It's been around for a long time. In 1982 Nieder-Ohmen celebrated its twelve-hundredth anniversary. Hard to believe! Many customs in the village dated back to the Middle Ages. In *Words That Burn Within Me,* my cousin Hilda wrote that every afternoon a man in uniform, the town crier, came around shaking his bell. Children would run up to find out what was going on. He called out the news of the day and then went on throughout the village. Anything the mayor wanted the village to know, the town crier would announce. Even though there was a newspaper in Giessen, the closest city, the local news was not covered in the press.

The town crier is no more. They now have radio, television and the Internet. In today's Nieder-Ohmen, there are no Jewish families. We visited the Jewish cemetery, which has been beautifully restored by the townspeople, and said *Kaddish* (the prayer for the dead) for my grandparents.

Heinrich has made it his mission to tell the stories of the Jews who lived in Nieder-Ohmen. He tracked down those of us who survived and documented those who perished in the Holocaust. Mr. Reighel researched the genealogy of the Stern family; and I now know more about my background than I ever did. He recently sent me his 185-page book that is a comprehensive history of Jewish life in Nieder-Ohmen

When I was young, Heinrich lived next door to us. He was ten years older than I, and used to light the fires in our house on Saturdays when Jews were not supposed to work. He remembers my mother giving him matzohs on Passover and making split pea soup for him when he was sick. He told me that my Aunt Rifka, my mother's nemesis who lived in the small flat upstairs in our house, would read him animal stories. His aunt, Anna, took me sledding in the moonlight.

There were good people in Nieder-Ohmen in the thirties, who were frightened and chose to stay silent. There are good people in Nieder-Ohmen today, and they are thinking about ways to combat anti-Semitism and educate the youth. May their thoughtfulness and their efforts lead to a future in which we can appreciate our differences and recognize our common humanity.

# Epilogue

- My Life Journey
- Lessons Learned
- Concluding Thoughts

# My Life Journey

Grandchildren Shira Inbar, Maya Inbar,
Katie Shenon, Rob Shenon, and Yotam Inbar (1996)

I am writing *An Accidental American* at the age of seventy-six. Friends have suggested you readers might want to know what happened to me after those first ten turbulent years. So, I decided to write a short life story. If you're interested, read on.

By my eleventh birthday, I was starting to feel like a REAL American. My friends, Barbara, Fern, and I would sit on Fern's front porch and sing songs from *Your Hit Parade* (the weekly magazine that had the lyrics of the top forty hit songs in it). Or, we might walk to Douglas Park and play ping pong in the recreation center. Riding a bike was out of the question. It cost too much money, but even if we could have afforded it, I suspect my mother would have said a resounding "NO!" After all, she did not allow me to roller skate because she was afraid I would fall down and get hurt. Paying for a broken arm would have been a serious problem for the Stern family.

I skipped from sixth grade to eighth grade in school with no adverse effects. Coming from an immigrant German background in which following the rules was stressed, I was used to doing my work and doing it well. I was a "goody goody" girl—completing my assignments, paying attention, and staying out of trouble.

John Marshall High School was an enormous red brick three-story building that covered a square block—a typical urban high school of its time. I had just turned thirteen when I first walked into Marshall High. The great masses of students rushing down locker-lined halls between classes and the noise they made—talking, laughing, shouting—overwhelmed me at first. Once I figured out where my classes were held and where the cafeteria was, I was okay.

We each had a locker for our books and coats. No backpacks in those days. One way to make friends was to talk to the kids whose lockers were near yours. Finding friends was complicated. There were strong divisions between the jocks, the grinds (serious students), the music and drama crowd, and, yes, there were even some dopers. You may not believe this, but after school, I'd often see a man in a dark overcoat, who sold "reefers" to the boys, lurking near the school entrance. I didn't know "reefers" were marijuana cigarettes, but I knew they were illegal and bad for you.

Clothes were important in high school. The popular girls had cashmere sweater sets and plaid pleated skits. I wanted some pretty clothes, too. So, I found after school and Saturday jobs. My first job was taking care of a bratty little boy in back of his parents' store. Trying to keep him from disturbing the customers was hard thankless work. I decided to look elsewhere and found a sales job in a "five-and-ten-cent" store near my house. Legally, workers were supposed to be sixteen years old before they could get a job there, but they hired me at thirteen. No one checked birth certificates. The small salary meant I, too, could buy a cashmere sweater set—only one—but that was better than none. When I became sixteen, I was hired by Sears and sold men's' shoes in the bargain basement. Many of the customers were amusing characters, and they liked buying their work boots from a young girl. We laughed a lot.

High school jobs taught me about everyday working class Chicagoans—useful information for later life. But, working daily after school kept me from most extra-curricular activities. However, I did get good grades, and as a result, I was elected president of the National Honor Society. At the ceremony, I was supposed to light three candles. I remember practicing lighting candles in the kitchen sink because I was worried that I wouldn't be able to light them properly, and the other kids would laugh at me.

Even with a cashmere sweater set, I was never a "popular" girl. I never dated basketball players (the big heroes in our school) or hung around with the rich kids, a few of whom drove cars to school. I hated gym class, especially when we played volleyball. The two team captains would get to choose their team, and, invariably, I'd be one of the last to be chosen. There was a good reason. I was a terrible player, but it still hurt my feelings. In later life, when we'd be at a picnic, and there was a volleyball game. I would not play, no matter how much my friends pleaded with me. Too many bad memories.

One bright spot in my high school career was having Miss Antmann for sophomore English. Her father had been wealthy and lost all his money in the Great Depression. He had taught his daughter, "People can take away from you what you have, but they can't take away from you what you are." It was Ms. Antmann's mission to turn us into cultured appreciators of the arts. Every quarter, we were required to do two cultural achievements—go to a concert, play, or opera. Since teenagers could usher in most concert halls and theaters, and public transportation was cheap for us, we were able to accomplish these assignments. What a thrill it was to see Victor Herbert's operetta *The Red Mill* at Chicago's grand opera house and watch my first Shakespeare play, *King Lear*, at Loyola University! Ms. Antmann opened up my ability to enjoy the arts in the same way Mrs. Anderson had opened up my awareness of the beautiful city in which I lived. Another great gift! Teachers have truly enriched my life. I am very grateful.

What was I going to do after high school?? That was a big question. My mother thought I should take a secretarial course. After all, secretaries can always find work. A marvelous thing happened! Both the University of Illinois at Champaign-Urbana and Roosevelt College, now known as Roosevelt University, offered me scholarships. Since Mama wouldn't hear of my leaving Chicago, I attended Roosevelt College, a streetcar college on Michigan Avenue in downtown Chicago.

Jewish teenagers stayed home from school on Jewish holidays. When I was a high school senior, my girlfriends and I strolled down Douglas Boulevard on *Rosh Hashonah* (the Jewish New Year) at the same time Burt Gasten and his boyfriends were doing the same thing. One of my friends knew one of his friends, and we all stopped and chatted. The rest is history.

Burt was a freshman at Illinois Institute of Technology (IIT), and was studying physics. He commuted to IIT's South Side campus by public transportation, which took about three hours a day. When we first met, I was going to high school and working after school. The following year, I started college and continued working after school.

There wasn't much spare time in our lives. We saw each other once a week for a Saturday night date. When Burt graduated four years later, we married on June 27, 1954, in a traditional Jewish wedding at the Sheridan Plaza Hotel surrounded by family and friends.

We started our married life with a move to Madison, Wisconsin, where Burt had been accepted for the Ph.D. program in physics at the University of Wisconsin. My practical mother had insisted that I take typing and shorthand classes in high school "just in case you ever need a job." Boy! Was that a good idea! I found a job as a secretary to the head of Superior Mutual Insurance Company, a high-risk auto insurance carrier. The joke around the office was "We insure the physically and mentally infirm."

When Burt was close to getting his Ph.D., I gave birth to Amy Lynn on July 24, 1961. She had big dark brown eyes that sparkled when she smiled. I fell totally in love with her and my new role as a mother. I read all the parenting books I could get my hands on and was determined to give her more love and security than I had as a child.

Lawrence Livermore National Laboratory was the place Burt decided was the best fit for his professional skills. The fact that his brother, Gene worked there, too, was a plus. I still remember February 22, 1962, the day we flew to California from Madison, Wisconsin. The nighttime temperature in Madison had been dropping to twenty degrees below zero for the past week. When we arrived in Livermore, the tulips were in bloom, and the temperature was about 65. Wow! We thought we'd died and gone to heaven!

We bought a tract house in Livermore, a used Chevy station wagon and started replacing our Salvation Army thrift store furniture with some new pieces. Three years later Felicia Ann was born, a tiny six-pound baby with blue eyes and fair skin. For a long time her nickname was "Teensy." My mother was overjoyed. Now her daughter was living the American Dream—two children, a house in the suburbs and a station wagon.

Livermore had a population of about 23,000—the size of a Chicago neighborhood. Burt got to know members of the City Council, many of whom worked at the Laboratory. We both became involved in local political campaigns—Burt, who was handy, by making campaign signs and distributing them, and I, who was gabby, by knocking on doors to talk to residents about the candidates we were supporting.

Burt had another talent that helped us make friends. He was able to fix anything! When that gift became known, our garage usually housed a broken toaster or television set awaiting his skilled attention.

Because I had the injunction "Do your vork!" firmly engraved in my brain, I started looking around for "vork" to do. It didn't take long to find some.

I joined the Nursery School Scholarship Fund, which raised money to send low income and non-English speaking children to local pre-schools. When President Johnson started the nationwide Head Start program, we applied to join it. One evening I missed going to a meeting. The next morning, I got a phone call telling me, "Ruth, you've been elected president of the Board." We called ourselves Community Association for Preschool Education. For the next three years CAPE was a big part of my life. I liked the fact that low-income kids went to many different schools in the valley (Livermore, Pleasanton, and Dublin) instead of being sent to one Head Start school.

My parents had now retired and moved to Livermore. This was a big help to me. Whenever I had an afternoon meeting, my father would ride his bike to my house and look after the children.

My other volunteer passion has been the Student Education Loan Fund, SELF, an organization that issues interest free loans to any Livermore student who wants further training after high school, whether it be a university, auto mechanics school, or beauty college. You know how important education is to us immigrants!

Livermore was filled with accomplished, talented women. On Wednesday afternoons, both of my daughters had Campfire Girl meetings, and I ran what I called "Ruth's Salon." A group of diverse talented women—young and old—would gather in my living room. The person who liked music might play a piece she had just learned. Someone who recently went to a workshop might talk about what had happened. It was the seventies when women were spreading their wings and searching for new horizons. The Salon was a place to share our interests and our lives. Being with these bright, educated women gave me the impetus to go back to college and finish my degree. In 1976 I finally received my BA in Public Service from the University of San Francisco.

By this time, I had been teaching parenting classes in Pleasanton and Livermore for the last seven years, an outgrowth of my work with CAPE. I attended a personal growth workshop conducted by Dr. James Carothers, who invited me to work with him. Our collaboration resulted in over ten years of workshops to help adults and children build self-esteem and the book, *Helping Children to Like Themselves*, which I talk about in *An Accidental American*.

Gasten family life was busy—filled with the activities of two growing girls, the occasional squabbles over toys, and then, later, the fights over who borrowed whose sweater. There were also weekend outings to the ocean or the mountains, and camping in Oregon with friends. In high school Amy became interested in the business world, but was uncertain about which part of it she wanted to study. My Uncle Leo from South Africa invited her to live there for a year and work in various departments of his hardware company to decide what aspects of commerce appealed to her. She took him up on his offer and left for Johannesburg, South Africa in September of 1979. We were excited for her, but hated having her so far away.

Everything changed on March 12, 1980, when Burt had a fatal heart attack while he was outside fixing the brakes on our Toyota sedan. Amy rushed home from South Africa. Amy, Felicia and I clung together in total shock, but secure in the knowledge that we had each other. Felicia was a sophomore at Livermore High School, and Amy enrolled at Las Positas College to major in accounting.

It's still hard to write about what happened next in our lives. On May 23, 1981, Felicia was killed in a car accident. The car was driven by one of her friends from school, Mike, who had restored the van with his father. Five young people were in the car when it went over an embankment. Felicia and Mike were in the front seat and died. The three teens in the back seat survived with minor injuries.

What to say about the next year? Amy and I somehow got through it with lots of help from our family and friends. I remember spending Thanksgiving sitting on the floor of the family room with Amy and my niece, Linda Gasten, eating nachos and listening to Beatles music. We couldn't face a traditional Thanksgiving although we had many invitations. A few days later, thanks to my Uncle Leo, we flew to South Africa and spent five weeks visiting with my uncles' families and taking a deluxe bus tour of that beautiful country. The change of scenery and the warm visits with family were a tonic for our spirits. When we returned home, Amy went back to college and I went tack to teaching parenting classes and conducting self-esteem workshops.

Amy met Michael Shenon, a tall, handsome recent University of California-Berkeley graduate at a workshop in San Francisco. They fell in love and married on June 28, 1987, at a beautiful outdoor wedding at the Elliston Winery in Sunol, followed by a joyful reception at the Castlewood Country Club in Pleasanton. Mike is one of five siblings, and his family warmly accepted Amy. I am glad she now has two sisters by marriage.

Two years later, on January 1, 1989, I married Ervin Chapman Woodward III, a kind, intelligent man of unusually diverse interests, also widowed, with whom I shared many friends. The Rabbi who performed our wedding jokingly told the guests, "It's not very often that I first perform a wedding ceremony for the daughter, and then two years later perform a wedding ceremony for the mother." A week before the wedding, I had gone for a routine physical and discovered that I had breast cancer. We told the family, but no one else, and went through the day with a secret burden in our hearts. On January 3, I had a mastectomy and soon afterwards started six month of chemotherapy. We postponed our planned honeymoon, a trip to Turkey, until June. I am happy to report that the cancer has been in remission for twenty-one years. Thank goodness!

Marrying Erv brought with it the pleasure of getting to know his son, Beau, and his son's partner, Tomoko, and his son, Paul, his wife, Yael, and their three engaging children, Shira, Maya, and Yotam. Mike and Amy added two more happily welcomed grandchildren, Katie and Rob, to our growing family. Erv and I lived a fulfilling life together, traveling and spending time with our children and grandchildren. When Erv died on January 15, 2000, it was a terrible blow to me, our blended family, and all who knew him.

Possibly caused by the stress of his death—or maybe not—I developed ovarian cancer in February 2001, which necessitated surgery and more chemotherapy. For the past nine years, I have been in remission. I am thankful.

As I write this, I realize you might think my life sounds pretty grim. Not true at all! Sure, my life has had its sorrows, but it has also had many joys, accomplishments, laughter, and allowed me to explore the beauty of much of the world. I continue teaching a few classes, which gives me a chance to be with young people—something I relish. I love talking to and listening to my grandchildren. A dear friend of Erv's, Sam Stone, has become my partner. If the universe cooperates, he and I will chaperone granddaughter Katie and three of her friends on a Mexican cruise to celebrate their graduations. Doesn't that sound like fun? The Jews have a toast—*L'Chaim!* (To LIFE!) My goal is to live LIFE with ZEST for as long as I can!

# Lessons Learned

I've been asked, "Well, what have you learned in your life that you'd like to share with your readers? Goodness! What a responsibility!

Here are the ones that come to mind today:

**1st Lesson: Go for the guy, not the car.**

How I learned it: When I was about 18, I thought the 1955 Thunderbird two seat sports car was the coolest car ever. I went on a date with a guy who owned one. He turned out to be boring and stupid. Maybe that's when I started liking smart men!

**2nd Lesson: Vote! Get involved in elections. Write letters! Support your candidate.**

How I learned it: In 1952, I was an eager volunteer for an organization that supported Adlai Stevenson, the brilliant Illinois

Governor, for president. I worked at the Democratic Convention and saw the political process at work. What a great learning experience!

## 3rd Lesson: If you take care of yourself, you benefit those around you.

How I learned it: When I was writing *Helping Children to Like Themselves*, I was so focused that I ignored a nagging toothache, which turned out to be an abscessed tooth. With an infection and lots of stress, I turned into a short-tempered demon. Amy and Felicia let me know how nasty I was by calling me "The Dragon Lady" and buying me ceramic and glass dragons. Wish I hadn't done that!

## 4th Lesson: When you're feeling terrible, remember you will feel better later.

How I learned it: After my daughter Felicia died, I thought I could never be happy again. One evening in San Francisco, I saw a beautiful sunset and, to my amazement, realized I felt happy. I still missed Felicia and always will, but I became aware that you can suffer a terrible loss and have happy moments in spite of it.

**5th Lesson: *Choose* to love your partner.**
How I learned it: I grew up thinking you fell in love and lived happily after. A friend said, "I choose to love my wife." I realized I can make a daily choice to love someone and act on it.

**6th Lesson: When something that seems important or life altering happens to me, I ask myself "What can I learn from this?"**
How I learned it: When I was diagnosed with breast cancer, I did some research and discovered exercise is a good way to stay healthy. So, I started exercising, reluctantly, I'll admit. It's now become part of my life, and I do it because it keeps me flexible and strong. And then, I discovered dancing,—both exercise *and* pleasure. What a find! I've had some challenging life experiences, as does everyone, sooner or later, and I've tried to make the best of them.

My favorite quotation is by Hillel, the Jewish sage.
IF I AM NOT FOR MYSELF, WHO WILL BE FOR
ME?
IF I AM ONLY FOR MYSELF, WHAT AM I?
IF NOT NOW, WHEN?

# Concluding Thoughts

Writing this book has been a revelation to me. I'm amazed to see how much of the immigrant child mentality still affects my behavior today. I still love those foods I first tasted when I came to America—thick corned beef sandwiches on rye, crisp juicy dill pickles, and delicately flavored smoked fish. On Tuesdays, I still check the grocery ads for the best buys for the week. I still buy most of my clothes on sale. I don't throw things out because I might need them someday. You'd laugh if you saw my garage.

On a more serious note, I grew up feeling that the German authoritarian way I was brought up didn't turn me into a young person with self-confidence and the ability to think for myself. As an adult, I studied child development and parenting strategies so that I could do a better job with my yet unborn children. So, that's how I found my life's work. Just think! It all happened because I didn't like the way my hardworking, well-meaning mother raised me.

I am filled with gratitude to live in this land where I first struggled and then thrived. I had the chance to take the values of my parents—hard work, importance of education, integrity—and use them to go on and develop as a person because I didn't live in a country that kept me "in my place." I hope that you, too, dear reader, will seize the opportunities offered to you and run with them. Good luck!

Get Published, Inc!
Thorofare, NJ 08086
18 March, 2010
BA2010077